MUSINGS

OF A

PERSECUTED SOUL

Mark Ewing

ISBN 978-1-0980-6213-2 (paperback)
ISBN 978-1-0980-6214-9 (digital)

Copyright © 2020 by Mark Ewing

All rights reserved. No part of this publication may be reproduced, distributed, or transmitted in any form or by any means, including photocopying, recording, or other electronic or mechanical methods without the prior written permission of the publisher. For permission requests, solicit the publisher via the address below.

Christian Faith Publishing, Inc.
832 Park Avenue
Meadville, PA 16335
www.christianfaithpublishing.com

Cover photo taken from the "The Last Judgment" panel of the Sistine Chapel in the Vatican City, Italy, painted by Michelangelo, circa 1512 AD.

Printed in the United States of America

Contents

Personal Introduction 5
Personal Reflection 8
Personal Reflection (Continued) 10
The Jewish Record 11
The Concept of Hell 13
The Concept of Hell (Continued) 15
Walking with God 17
Education 19
Education (Continued) 21
What Is Faith? 23
Does God Heal Amputees? 25
Does God Heal Amputees? (Continued) 27
The Precepts of God 29
Are We Predestined to Heaven or Hell? 31
Are We Predestined to Heaven or Hell? (Continued) 33
The Big Bang Theory 34
The Big Bang Theory (Continued) 36
Kicking Against the Goads 37
The Mystery of God 39
Spiritual Peace 41
Pathways to Prayer 43
Prayer Warrior 45
The Concept of Eternal Security 47
The Concept of Eternal Security (Continued) 49
The Twenty-third Psalm 50
The Tribulation Controversy 52
The Rapture 54
End-Time Sequence of Events 56

Sanctification 57
Sanctification (Continued) 59
Communion with God 60
Why Do Calamities Happen? 62
What Is the Essence of Faith? 64
The Mystery of the Holy Spirit 66
The Mystery of the Holy Spirit (Continued) 68
Reconciliation 70
Can Prayer Alter God's Will? 72
Can Prayer Alter God's Will (Continued) 74
Carnality and the Cross 75
Spiritual Joy 77
The Gift of Israel 79
The Gift of Israel (Continued) 81
Final Thoughts 82

Personal Introduction

The following writings were originally started as a spiritual legacy for my two sons, but I was writing with a deep ache in my soul. As a lifelong Christian, I have experienced a broad spectrum of religious dogma, from the "frozen chosen" of Calvinism to "let's tape everyone here speaking in tongues" of the charismatic movement that swept through my family in the early 1970s. I have also, unfortunately, witnessed the spiritual collapse of many Christians that I held in high esteem. These personal experiences led to a judgmental cynicism of many aspects of accepted Christian dogma. I was aware of these feelings, but I did little to change them. When I started to write *Musings* I was in this dark place. Remarkably, over a period of months as I researched and wrote, I began to notice a change in my perception. The cynicism that had long governed my thinking was slowly replaced with a peace that I had not felt for decades. I attribute this to the Holy Spirit, who, unbeknownst to me, was using my scriptural research in the Bible to work a spirit of repentance within me. Hebrews 4:12 defines this process beautifully. "The Word of God is living and powerful and sharper than any two-edged sword, piercing even to the dividing asunder of soul and spirit and of the joints and marrow, and is a discerner of the thoughts and intents of the heart." As this spiritual healing was occurring, I began praying "as a child," asking the Holy Spirit to intercede for me, as I did not know how to approach the Throne of God. Writing and researching for additional topics in *Musings* became a wonderful refreshing experience for me. Over the course of my writings, I have shared my simple thoughts with many others, some who are believers and some who are not. I have been blessed with the lively interaction and debate that such discussions bring. We can all benefit from expanding our understanding of the great mysteries of God through the guidance of the Holy Spirit. You probably won't agree with all of my opinions, but if *Musings* causes you to renew your own spiritual life through scriptural research, as it did for me, then we both can give God the glory.

In 1969, when I was eighteen years old and in my first year of college, I was introduced to a Renaissance art class. We studied the frescos on the ceiling of the Sistine Chapel in Italy, which were painted by Michelangelo over five hundred years ago. In one of these paintings, God is seen presiding over the Last Judgment of mankind. Those individuals not found in the Book of Life are being condemned to eternal punishment in hell. For some reason, my eyes fell upon one individual out of hundreds in the fresco. This man had received his final judgment from God, and the demons of Hell are reaching out to take him. His face portrays such anguish, as he realizes the missed opportunities he had to accept God throughout his life, and having failed to do so, now faces his eternal fate. That tortured face has haunted me for years. In Philippians 2:12, we are told to "work out our salvation with fear and trembling." When the Last Trump blows, when our life on this Earth is over and our eternal state begins, each of us will receive judgment. If we are saved, our judgment is adjudicated through Jesus Christ. If we are not saved, that judgment condemns without mercy. Now is the appointed time. It is my earnest prayer that your life reflects the grace of God through Jesus Christ.

Personal Reflection

I start this treatise on a personal note. As a steward of Christ's great commission (Matt. 28), God's explicit command for Christians to spread the Gospel, I have struggled. It may be said that this hesitancy on my part is due to shallowness in my commitment to Christ. There is some truth to this, but I am not alone. A recent study based on survey data from people who identify themselves as Christians concluded that as high as 90 to 95 percent had not shared Christ with a nonbeliever. My empathy for other people has always been tempered in the crucible of my personal experiences. There have been times in my life where I felt great spiritual awareness, keenly seeking God's daily guidance with "mountaintop" clarity. I have also experienced periods of "drought" where I felt spiritually dried up. I have unfortunately witnessed the spiritual downfall of Christian leaders, leaving me with a cynicism toward "super-charged" evangelists. Philippians 4:5 comes to mind: "Let your moderation be known to all men." It is because of my life experiences that I suffer from what's called the "duality of man." My Christian upbringing frequently butts up against my secular education and personal observations of the natural world. My belief in Jesus as Savior is grounded through the historicity of the Bible and its prophetic writings. The remarkable story of the Jewish people and the reemergence of the State of Israel stand in my opinion as irrefutable proof for the validity of Old Testament prophesies. It seems that whenever I find myself leaning toward a unitarian approach to religion, I cannot silence that quiet inner voice that whispers, "Look to Jerusalem and behold the truth of my ways." That does not say that challenges don't present themselves to my belief system. As a naturalist by education, I lean toward a liberal understanding of the physical world. I believe that through the process of evolution, vast changes can occur in living organisms over time. I am convinced that the Earth is geologically ancient. I believe that there is evidence of modern man's existence on this Earth that dates back thirty to fifty thousand years. I do not believe that dinosaurs and man walked the Earth at the same time. I say these things to differentiate myself from those who believe in a strict literal interpretation of all scripture, including the Genesis record. Christians have been philosophically divided on this issue for ages. The traditional church perspective has leaned heavily toward literal interpretation, where the record of uninterrupted human lineage listed in Genesis chapters 4–5 and Matthew chapter 1 restricts the age of the Earth to approximately six thousand years. This is not a time frame that I wish to squeeze the Earth's geologic evidence into. Do we, as Christians, close a blind eye to such issues, or do we have the courage to openly discuss areas of the Bible that raise certain levels of uneasiness in our spirit? The reality of Jesus allows me to examine my Christian ideology and hopefully find spiritual equilibrium.

Personal Reflection (Continued)

These writings represent my search for spiritual equilibrium. It is my layman's attempt to find answers to questions frequently promulgated by the nonbelieving world. People of secular ideology often refute the veracity of the Bible, citing as evidence such stories as Noah's Ark, Jonah and the Whale, and the creation account in the book of Genesis. Most Christians find themselves ill-prepared to engage in these discussions. In *Musings*, I will endeavor to put on the whole Armor of God (as described in Ephesians 6:13), and through the use of the Sword of the Spirit (the Bible), try to find answers to queries such as these. The renowned evangelist Billy Graham, late in his life, began to have doubts pertaining to the church doctrine of eternal punishment for unbelievers. When his concerns became known, he was strongly attacked, with some in the Christian community going so far as to label him a "false teacher," so I tread lightly in these waters. My writing points are not an attempt to undermine established religious precedent. It's simply to start dialog. The books of the Bible, written over the course of several thousand years and authored by many, are remarkable in their cohesive message of God's intent and purpose for mankind. Prophetically perfect in every detail, the Word of God is faithfully positioned to provide answers to many of these nagging questions. So let's talk about it.

The Jewish Record

I believe the historicity of the Bible is grounded in the Jewish record. The books of the Old Testament chronicle an amazing journey of a people, who, through genealogy, represent an unbroken lineage to the prophesied Messiah (Jesus). The descendants of Abraham and Sarah (Genesis 17:19) would assimilate throughout the world's nations and cultures in the millennia to follow, stubbornly adhering to the Mosaic laws and rituals established by God over 3,500 years ago. Jesus, as Messiah, was prophesied to be born into this distinct bloodline, arising from the stem of Jesse (Isaiah 11:1). His manner of birth, life, ministry, and death were documented in Old Testament prophesies. As with Jesus, God's specific blessing for his chosen people was clearly indicated in scripture (Genesis 12:2). At the time of this blessing, the Israelites were a ragtag Bedouin-style desert people without their own land. The destiny of this stubborn race of people would soon change. With God's blessing, they became a fierce tribe of warriors with far-minded leaders who kept their eye on the fiery pillar that pointed them to the promised land. As long as they were obedient to God, his mercies rained from heaven, but obedience was a heavy yoke to bear. As Israel descended into idol worship and debauchery, God removed his protection, and the Israelites soon found themselves conquered, enslaved, and cast to the far ends of the Earth. Although banished from the land of milk and honey, God never withdrew the special blessing he had promised to Abraham. For generations to come, Jewish proclivity for intellectual thought and achievement transcended all boundaries in philosophy, music, finance, physics, medicine, and the arts. This success, however, came at great personal cost. Through the centuries that followed, pogroms centered on anti-Semitism fomented prejudice and outright loathing, horrifically culminating in 1940 with Hitler's attempt to eradicate, by genocide, the entire Jewish population in Europe during World War II. Six million people of Jewish descent were systematically murdered in concentration camps. Their properties and accumulated wealth vanished forever into the coffers of the Nazi war machine. Old Testament prophesies warn that anti-Semitism will bring God's retribution (Genesis 12:3), and the complete destruction of the German nation and her people at the end of WWII is stark evidence of this warning. This same retribution is seen today, visited on nations that align themselves against the State of Israel. When one examines the historical context of Jewish contributions to human society, it becomes undeniably clear that in his infinite wisdom, God chose to bless his people with an intellectual advantage. A people gifted with reasoning power will rise to leadership positions in all aspects of society. Dating back to the time of Jacob (Genesis 30:25), this superiority of intellect can be observed through his ability to use genetic breeding selection in cattle, sheep, and goats. This amazing gift continues today when one considers that Jews have been awarded nearly 30 percent of all Nobel Prizes since 1950. People of Jewish heritage comprise only 2 percent of the United States population but make up almost one third of all students accepted to elite universities. Jewish doctors, lawyers, and financial leaders often make up a majority of the professional population in many modern countries. Far more remarkable are the findings of research studies performed on racial intelligence. The Ashkenazi Jews rank at the top of the leader board, a full 40 percent higher than average world IQ. This blessing of intellect has well-served the descendants of Abraham and Sarah, securing their seat on the world's stage and placing them, unwittingly, in the crosshairs of cataclysmic world events to come.

The Concept of Hell

In the preceding pages, I have proffered my layman's examination of the Jewish record in its prophetic validation of the Old Testament. Another topic for discussion is the concept of hell, a place of torment for the wicked. Jesus often spoke on this subject, and in Matthew 10:28, he warned of the "destruction" of both body and soul in hell. The concept of a hellish eternity for the lost was officially fomented during the fourth century AD by Augustine of Hippo, a significant church theologian, who postulated that every human soul was immortal and, therefore, must spend eternity in either heaven or hell. Augustine's premise was embraced by the Roman Church and later by the Protestant Reformation and has remained as an integral teaching in church canon for centuries. Scripture clearly states that God will grant immortality, i.e., eternal life to the souls of believers after death. This was first described in Genesis 3:22, in terms of eating from the tree of life, but when Adam and Eve disobeyed, their idyllic status with God was terminated. Sin brings punishment, and through their sin, Adam and Eve were banished from the Garden and denied access to the tree of life. Long before Adam, however, sin had found its place in the universe through a different act of defiance. Matthew 25:41 states that hell, the "place of everlasting fire," was actually prepared for Satan and his fallen angels. When Adam brought human sin into the world, hell as punishment was expanded to include those not found in the Book of Life (Revelation 20:15). Scripture is not ambiguous in its description of this final place of the damned, so what does scripture actually say about the length of that punishment? In Luke chapter 16, Jesus presents the parable of Lazarus, where the environment of hell is graphically described, but Jesus does not state that the rich man will suffer there for all eternity.

There is only one verse in the Bible that explicitly states a never-ending conscious state of hellish torment for human souls. Found in the fourteenth chapter of Revelation verses 9–11, God decrees eternal punishment, in torment, for a very specific group of people. These are humans who, during the final years of the Tribulation, have willingly taken the mark of the beast (the Antichrist) and have actively worshiped Satan as god. Scripture does not define how large this group of people is, but clearly, they will suffer the same tormenting eternal fate that is reserved for Satan and his fallen angels.

The Concept of Hell (Continued)

After researching Bible passages pertaining to hell, my presumptive opinion leans toward some form of conscious punishment for the unsaved at the Final Judgment. A parable told by Jesus, recorded in the book of Luke, seems to indicate degrees of punishment in hell. Luke 12:46–48 describes a sequence of punishments called "stripes," which refers to lashes from a whip. The number of lashes to be administered is in accordance with the degree of malfeasance found in the individual. Revelation 20:13 also lends some credence to the theory of a measured punishment in hell by saying that the unsaved will be judged on their lives by an examination of a "book of works." This is similar to the Catholic doctrine of "purgatory," where saved people who have died must first "work off" their impurities before being granted admittance to heaven. The debate between traditionalists, who believe the unsaved soul will suffer conscious torment in hell for all eternity, and annihilationists, who believe that scripture points to soul destruction, not soul immortality, for the damned, has waged in the Christian church for centuries. Annihilationists believe that a merciful God will not punish sins committed in an earthly lifetime with a never-ending punishment in hell. Traditionalists see no moral conflict in this. Their defense for eternal punishment rests on the dimension of God's holiness, where sin cannot be tolerated. Hell, as a literal place, is scripturally supported in both Old and New Testaments. Luke chapter 16 describes the environment of hell in startling detail. Even if viewed as a parable, it portrays the anguish felt by the rich man in being there. The use of the Greek word "basanos" literally means tormented. This is the word Jesus chose to describe the rich man in hell, but basanos is only found twice in the New Testament. Far more frequently, the fate of the soul in hell is described by the Greek word "apollumi," which means destruction. A case can be made that the more common usage of "apollumi" indicates that the unsaved soul in the afterlife is not immortal. Throughout the Bible, the evidence of God's mercy and long-suffering is well-documented. In Genesis 18:25, Lot was able to barter with God concerning the fate of Sodom and Gomorrah. "Will not the Judge of all the earth do right?" Lot asked in their conversation over what constitutes "just punishment." As presumptuous as it sounds, Lot was seemingly able to procure an extended period of mercy for the inhabitants of those sinful cities. There are many such stories in the Bible where God was willing to stay his hand of righteous judgment if certain conditions were met. For Christians, this stay of punishment is grounded in the personal acceptance of Jesus as Savior. Jesus says in John 14:6, "I am the way, the truth and the life, no man cometh unto the Father but by me." There is no ambiguity in that statement. Outside Christ's saving grace, there is only bitter judgment to be faced by those who refused the salvation of the cross. The scriptural record is clear that they will be judged and suffer the torments of the lake of fire as punishment for their sins. The question rests on whether that punishment is eternal in its extent, or is it plausible, in the light of scriptural evidence, to believe that God will end their suffering at some point with final destruction (apollumi) of their souls?

Walking with God

In the first chapter of Genesis, verse 26, it states that God created man in his "image and likeness." This simple phrase holds the key to our understanding of the intellectual rift that exists between humans and all other animals. As the secular world struggles to explain how this obvious distinction came to be through the lens of a godless evolutionary process, Christians remain secure in the answer that at conception, we receive the breath of God in our nostrils. Within each one of us, there lies a seed of spiritual "awareness" that is not evident in any other form of life on the earth. Anthropological studies have found evidence of this "spirituality" in all known human societies, regardless of ethnicity, culture, or technological development. Man's creation in the "image and likeness" of God is a profound revelation, illuminating our unique purpose and place in the universe. God endowed mankind with spiritual acuity for the singular purpose of fellowship. This is clearly revealed in 2 Chronicles 7:14 where God says, "if my people, who are called by my name, shall humble themselves, and pray, and seek my Face, and turn from their sinful ways, then I will hear from heaven, and will forgive their sin, and will heal their land." Adam enjoyed unobstructed fellowship with God in the Garden until he allowed sin to enter his heart. Sin will always interfere with man's relationship to God. The biblical story of David, found in the books of Samuel, illustrates the effects of sin even on "a man after God's own heart" (Acts 13:22). In his youth, David found great favor with God, but he allowed himself to be tempted and drawn into great transgressions. David later repented before God, but he was never able to fully regain his intimacy before the Lord. If our fellowship with God falls primarily on Sunday mornings, we miss the central theme of God's intent when he breathed his breath into each of us. As former US Senate Chaplain Richard Halverson once said, "What matters is believing Jesus, not just our beliefs about Jesus." Chaplain Halverson was referring to a "realness" of fellowship that comes only through seeking God in everything we do. There will be times when we must petition our heavenly Father formally, going into our prayer closet as Jesus advised in Matthew 6:6, but our true fellowship is grounded through everyday interactions. As stated in 1 Chronicles 16:11, we must find ways to commune with God amid the daily clutter of life. It is in these simple innocuous musings with our Creator that the fellowship, faith, and trust of our relationship is anchored.

Education

Education is a blessing, but sometimes it feels like a curse. We know through scriptures, such as John 12:31 that Satan is prince of the earthly realm. In 2 Corinthians 4:4, he is called the deceiver of man. Satan uses every conceivable medium, including education, to effectuate his pogrom against God. For most Americans, the educational journey begins in kindergarten and continues through a conduit of secular schools until we graduate from high school or college. Reverence for God used to be an important part of the public education experience. This ended in 1962, when the US Supreme Court removed prayer from public schools. In doing so, the Court unwittingly adjudicated in favor of Satan, creating a secular educational system where he has a free reign to mislead, beguile, and cast doubt into young people's thinking concerning the existence of God. I am the product of both Christian and secular school systems. I received my education in zoology at the University of Iowa, where there was no credence given, whatsoever, to the creation theory. Secular evolution of all life forms, including man, was presented through the godless prism of humanism. Students were taught that humans evolved from the lower primates by simple luck in the genetic lottery of DNA mutations. In 1859, Charles Darwin published a book titled *On the Origin of Species*, which tendered a new way of thinking about how life began on Earth. In order to explain the diversification of species, Darwin's theory relied on a "secular change agent," rather than a Creator. This proposal of "godless creation" was not well-received by the public in the mid-1800s. I am reminded of a scene in the movie *Gettysburg* where Confederate General George Pickett was engaged in a campfire debate over Darwin's theory. He abruptly ended the argument by "personally challenging" anyone who believed that the ancestors of General Robert E. Lee were descendants of apes. In Darwin's time, the DNA genetic molecule was unknown, so in order for his theory to work, he needed to find a process, which would enable an organism to pass on any adaptations to the next generation. A classic Darwinian explanation for this evolutionary process can be found in a study of the giraffe's long neck. The fossil record of the giraffe, over millions of years, shows a substantial lengthening of its neck. To explain this change, Darwin proposed that in each generation, a giraffe's neck became minutely longer through stretching to feed on higher branches, and over the course of its reproductive life, this adaptation was passed on to its offspring. Over time, this would result in each new generation of giraffes having slightly longer necks and would ultimately be reflected in the fossil record. To put this in human perspective, Darwin's explanation would allow a body builder's massive physique, developed over years of heavy weight training, to be passed on to his children. This proposal of Darwin's was obviously incorrect, but it remained a mainstay of evolutionary thought until 1952 when the DNA molecule was discovered. The genetic code on the DNA molecule is fairly stable, but occasionally, it does mutate, and when it does, there are effects on the organism. The great majority of these effects are harmful, but given enough time, some mutations occur that assist the organism to survive. These "good changes" will be passed down to offspring. Darwin's theory of "survival of the fittest" where nature eliminates the weaker organisms, coupled with a genetic code that mutates, provides scientists with a secular model for explaining the evolution of life on Earth. There is one key ingredient, however, that is necessary to make evolution work. Species evolution through random DNA mutation is an incredibly slow process and is only achievable if eons of time are placed into the geologic formula.

Education (Continued)

When asked about the age of the Earth, most people will agree that it appears to be very old. The concept of ancient life begins early in the minds of children through drawings of dinosaur pictures, or visits to museums, where enormous fossil skeletons are on display. In grade school, students are taught about immense geologic forces at work including plate tectonics, which slide entire continents very slowly over the Earth's surface. Personal observations begin to solidify this ancient Earth concept. A visit to the Grand Canyon exposes one's senses to the awe-inspiring work of nature's erosional forces over time. In NYC's central park, people can walk over rocks where glacial scrape marks of the last Ice Age are still visible. Museums, such as the La Brea Tar Pits in Los Angeles, allow the visual inspection of massive skeletons of extinct land mammals such as the saber-toothed tiger and wooly mammoth. The physical signs of an ancient Earth are literally all around us. From a Christian standpoint, however, this evidence may present a conundrum. If we firmly hold to the Genesis account of creation, which is based on a sixday period and starting with Adam, the geologic age of the Earth can be no older than six thousand years. This time frame does not sync with what we have been taught in school, or with what we have personally observed in the world. Some biblical scholars, such as C. I. Scofield, contend that Moses wrote this chapter as a generalized outline of creation, using phraseology that an uneducated man of that time period would understand. This proposal has substantiation in scriptures such as 2 Peter 3:8, where a "day" may represent a thousand years to the Lord. A "day" may also represent a billion years of God's evolutionary processes. As followers of Christ, we are not forced into making choices over the Earth's geologic age. Whether the cosmos was created six thousand years ago or four billion, should never be germane to one's evaluation of their belief in God. There's room for differences of interpretation in scripture, and this liberty allows our spiritual equilibrium to mature. This freedom, however, must be tendered carefully, for Satan's snares are set to entangle the unwary. For years, I did not accept, as verbatim, the stories of Jonah being swallowed by the whale, or Noah's great flood. I could find no evidence in the fossil record of a cataclysmic flood event less than four thousand years ago; neither could I conceive of a human being surviving in a marine creature's digestive tract for three days. For most of my adult life, I kept these stories shelved in the back corner of Biblical truth. To the unbeliever, many Old Testament stories are simply too incredible to believe on their scientific merit, and even Christians have been hardened by secular scientific teaching to disdain "miracles." Many of the story-wrapped truths in the Old Testament fall into this category. As believers in Christ, we can't ignore events written in the Old Testament, as they represent part of the inspired canon, but attempting to make logical sense out of these things can persecute one's soul. Jesus then enters, speaking to his disciples about Jonah's three-day experience in the belly of the great fish in Matthew 12:40 and Noah's flood in Matthew 24. To deny the veracity of Christ is a step too far for any Christian to go, and, therefore, we find ourselves positioned once again on the balance scale of "faith versus science." The Bible was not written to be in perfect alignment with our preconceived notions. It was written to be in perfect alignment with God's. We "see through the glass darkly," and it is by faith that we hold as truth the things that we can't perceive through our human understanding.

What Is Faith?

What is the essence of faith? Hebrews 11:1 defines faith as the substance of things hoped for, the evidence of things not seen. We cannot see God, but we are witness to the marvels of his handiwork all around us. Christians believe that Jesus was resurrected from the dead, and through faith in his resurrection, we have the hope of eternal life. In 1 Corinthians 15:17 the Apostle Paul states that if Christ was not raised from the dead, our faith would be worthless. New Testament's great exposition on faith is found in the eleventh chapter of the book of Hebrews. In verse 6 of that chapter, it states, "that without faith, it is impossible to please God, for he that cometh to God must first believe that God exists, and that he is a rewarder of them that diligently seek Him." That statement has no ambiguity. We must first have faith in God's existence and then he will reward those who seek after his truth. Jesus repeatedly blessed those who sought after him in faith. Luke 18:42 describes the blind man who was healed and received his sight because of his faith. Jesus marveled at the faith of the centurion who asked for his servant's healing. In Matthew 17:20, Jesus admonished his disciples for their failure to cast out demons, stating that it was their lack of faith that created the problem. "If ye had faith as small as a mustard seed, you could move mountains." The woman with an issue of blood for twelve years had faith that if she could just touch the hem of Jesus's garment, she would be healed. When she touched his hem, Jesus turned to her and said that her faith had made her well. Hebrews 14:6 states it is by faith that we may boldly approach the throne of grace to obtain mercy. Colossians 2:12 says we are risen with him through faith in the operation of God, who hath raised him from the dead. Our faith assures us that God is in control of every aspect of our lives, that he is truly our Father, whereby he is always faithful and just. We are therefore afforded the absolute assurance of his promises and blessings in our lives. Our faith is strengthened by the Holy Spirit (Romans 10:17), "for then faith cometh by hearing and hearing by the Word of God." God's desire is for each of us to grow in our faith that we may come to trust him in every aspect of our lives. Faith requires staunchness, a resolute commitment to the person of Jesus Christ, not just to our beliefs about Jesus. Faith releases Jesus from the dry consignment of stodgy religion and places him in rightful authority over our lives. Faith is sustained through prayer. Jesus promised that if we ask anything in his name, it shall be given to us in accordance with his will (1 John 5:14). Our faith is markedly strengthened when we receive definitive answers to prayer requests, but do we waiver when prayer requests are not tendered to our expectations? The answer to this question is found in 2 Corinthians 12:7–13 where the Apostle Paul prayed three times to have a physical infirmity healed. His requests before God were denied. Jesus told Paul that his healing was denied because Christ had a greater purpose for Paul's affliction. These denials are difficult to receive, but we must understand that just as our earthly fathers did not always give us everything we asked for, so also our heavenly Father must review our requests within the scope of his will. As we place our petitions before God in prayer, we have faith that our Father will hear them and will provide some form of answer to us. We must have faith to receive God's answer, whether be it yea or nay, with an understanding in our hearts that it is not our will, but his that matters.

Does God Heal Amputees?

Healing was an important aspect of Jesus's earthly ministry. There are at least thirty-eight documented events of healings by Jesus found in the Gospels. These healings were all performed openly and in the presence of witnesses, sometimes hundreds of witnesses. Even as Jesus performed these miracles, he knew that these healing manifestations would not be convincing proof of his authority. He spoke of this in Luke 16:31 when he said, "If they didn't believe Moses and the Prophets, neither will they be persuaded, though one rose from the dead." Although Jesus knew that performing healing miracles would not sway the populace, they were essential in sustaining the new faith of his disciples. I was reading a blog the other day from a self-proclaimed atheist that questioned why there are no documented cases of God healing amputees. The article was obviously written in an attempt to refute the veracity of Christ, but it piqued my interest because of my own father, who was stricken with polio at a young age. The disease left him totally paralyzed in both legs and one arm and confined him to life in a wheelchair for fifty years. Though a devout Christian, he never received physical healing from his paralysis, even though there were many attempts made by people in the Christian community to do so. The Bible gives instructions on how to seek physical healing in James 5:14–15. This passage says, "The prayer of faith shall save the sick." Do missing or paralyzed limbs qualify as a "sickness"? I don't have that answer. I do find it interesting that you never witness a TV evangelistic healer bring an amputee onto the stage for restoration of their limbs. Why is this? It would seem that the logical answer lies in provability. Most of the healings seen on TV can be explained through psychosomatic processes. The patient feels better because he is expecting to feel better, much like the result from taking a placebo pill. Restoring a missing arm or leg raises the miracle to a higher level altogether. So why did Jesus not select an amputee for healing, even though there must have been hundreds around him? Unlike the atheist, I do not seek an answer to this mystery through disbelief. Quite the contrary. As a believer, I endeavor to find scriptural answers for why God chose not to do this. In the synoptic gospels, such as in Matthew 17:20, Mark 11:24, or Matthew 18:19, Jesus talks about performing miracles through faith. Jesus frequently uses the term "if you believe in me." That is a faith statement. As Jesus spoke to his disciples about having the faith to move mountains, or cast out demons, or heal the sick, he was preparing them for the time after his ascension when the gospel message would rest on their shoulders. The phrase "if you believe in me" is key to receiving this power.

Does God Heal Amputees? (Continued)

In Matthew 16:4, Jesus rebukes the Pharisees when they were asking him for a sign that he was God. He responded by saying, "You seek after a sign, but no sign will be given you." God was intentionally withholding indisputable evidence of his power because of the hypocrisy in their hearts. Restoring an amputated leg is a healing miracle that stands on its own merit. It does not require faith to believe when one sees an arm restored. A further explanation to the "amputee" question may be found in 2 Corinthians 12:7–9. Apostle Paul authored approximately half of all the New Testament books. He was specifically called to be an apostle of Christ through a miraculous conversion experience. It is my belief that God chose Paul because of his unique qualifications for the challenge that would be put before him. Paul was articulate, he carried Roman citizenship, which allowed him to travel freely and safely throughout the Mediterranean, he was a Pharisee, and he was stubborn. We would call him "task-oriented" in today's vernacular. He became God's point man in the establishment of the new covenant throughout Asia Minor. Paul's faith in the Lord Jesus is unquestioned, and because of this, he was able to perform many miracles, which are recorded in the book of Acts. At some point in his ministry, however, he became seriously troubled by a physical affliction. Scriptures such as Galatians 4:13–15 and Galatians 6:11, seem to indicate that Paul's eyes were failing. This affliction was so aggravating to Paul that he petitioned to God for healing on three separate occasions. Surprisingly, these prayer requests for healing were denied. God provided Paul with the following explanation, "My grace is sufficient for thee, for my strength is made perfect in weakness." Paul's response was characteristic of his love and unwavering faith in Jesus and mirrors what my dad felt, "most gladly therefore, will I rather glory in my infirmity, that the Power of Christ may rest upon me" (2 Corinthians 12:9). Healing, therefore, is centered on an individual's faith and the will of God. In Luke 5:12, the leper said, "If thou will," and received healing. Jesus uttered these words in Luke 22:42, "Not my will, but thine be done." And Apostle John tells us in 1 John 5:14, "If we ask anything according to his will, He hears us." How much human faith is necessary to actually believe that an amputee will receive a new limb? Maybe more than we have.

The Precepts of God

Lately, I have been doing some research on the precepts of God. Our knowledge of God's identity is through the inspired writings of the Holy Bible. It is there we are made aware of God's omniscience, his immutability, and his position of absolute authority in the universe (Isaiah 46:9). Through faith, we have assurance that God's sovereignty will remain unchanged for all eternity. By his immutable design, the heavens were formed, and life, with its miracle of DNA, was established on Earth. In his authority, God foresaw the entire course of human history with its tragedy of sin, but his love and long-suffering for mankind would not alter. This complex relationship between God and man is best viewed through the historical record of the Jewish people. Judaism, an established religion for over 3,500 years, has persevered through centuries of intense persecution, ever obedient to its retention of ancient traditions, customs, celebrations, and language. Abraham's prodigy, gifted with God's blessing, would find themselves scattered among the world's populations, assimilating into cultures where secular ideology would have its insidious effect. Slowly, over time, the Jewish people turned away from the love relationship they once had with God, preferring to accept a more agnostic view of their place in history. Today, modern polling data confirms that the majority of Jewish people worldwide view themselves as secular in their religious beliefs. This same shift toward secularism is evidenced throughout the nonJewish world as well. For the last half century, Christian church membership has been experiencing a dramatic decline. The majority of Americans under the age of fifty have been relentlessly pounded by an anti-religious propaganda campaign promulgated through public schools, college campuses, and most egregiously, in the entertainment world. Over the last twenty years, the unregulated use of the Internet has played an increasingly destructive role in society. Its social media platforms have provided an unrestricted access for bullying and hateful speech and have been instrumental in the alarming rise of teen suicides. Pornography and other forms of filth that were once consigned to the back shelf of magazine racks have surreptitiously, through the home computer, slithered their way into virtually every American household. Faced with a progressively secular population, pastors have found themselves capitulating to demands for reform in the church. Too often, this reform movement has come at the expense of the Gospel message, favoring, instead, a less confrontive church environment. The secularization of our church environs leave parishioners unprepared for battle against Satan's snares and temptations (Ephesians 6:12). Scriptures warn against "lukewarm" churches that have given consent to a watered-down Gospel message (Revelation 3:16). God's sovereign will does not and will not change in respect to sin. Sin is abhorrent to a holy God. Only the blood of Jesus can wash sin away and that must occur through an act of personal repentance. 2 Peter 3:9 declares that he does not desire that any person should perish but that all should come to repentance. Our loving Lord came to Earth to save a sinful undeserving world through the ultimate sacrifice of himself. Christ's atonement on the cross is a love gift for everyone (Matthew 16:25, Mark 8:35). The decision to receive Christ, however, must be made by the individual through their free will to choose. It is by our own decisions, while we yet live, that our eternal status is determined. Human societies will evolve, churches will falter, but God remains forever on his throne. Therein lies the source of our greatest peace: in knowing that our heavenly Father is a God of holiness and love, and his sovereignty will endure forever.

Are We Predestined to Heaven or Hell?

Within the Christian community, a great debate has raged for nearly two thousand years. This disagreement played a prominent role in the rise of the Reformation movement of the 14th and 15th centuries. The controversy is over the doctrine of predestination. Martin Luther and John Calvin were the standard bearers for elucidating the concept of God foreordaining (controlling) everything in the universe, including the eternal destination of all mankind. For the first several centuries following Christ's resurrection, this doctrine of predestination was not embraced by the early church fathers and was not affirmed in Judaism at all. The rise of this doctrine to one of prominence in the church was initiated by Augustine of Hippo, who, in 430 AD, authored several letters promulgating that God, in his omniscience, predestined (chose), which souls would be saved and which would be damned. Augustine, if you remember from earlier pages in *Musings*, was the clergyman who was instrumental in promoting the concept of hell as a place of eternal conscious torment for the unbeliever. His writings were heavily influenced by Hellenistic philosophers such as Plato. The Roman Catholic Church did not ascribe to Augustine's presumption of predestination, much preferring the doctrine of man's "free will." These differing ideologies would come to blows during the Protestant Reformation nearly one thousand years later. In examining this issue, the Bible presents many scriptures that seem to support both doctrines. Even the twin pillars of the Protestant Reformation, Martin Luther and John Calvin, did not completely agree on the extent of God's predetermining the eternal status of man. Predetermination is a cold doctrine, and most

Christians experience a feeling of "unfairness" about it that is disconcerting. Taken to its extreme, the doctrine presents an image of God that few would find agreeable. For the redeemed soul, it matters little whether salvation comes through one's free will, or God's pre-choosing, but for the lost soul, one that faces an eternity in punishment, our hearts cry out for justification. When seeking truth in the Bible, it becomes clear there is a substantial body of scriptural evidence that, on the surface, seems to support Calvin's doctrine. Ephesians 1:4 says "that having been chosen by God from before the foundations of the world." In Romans 9:14–22, Apostle Paul discusses the fairness of the potter making vessels for glory and vessels for destruction, and Paul asks, "Who are we to judge the will of the potter?" These verses, and many others, seem to suggest a path of salvation other than our own free will, and if this is true, then what effect does that have on the purpose of Christ's atonement? On the flip side of the coin, the doctrine of man's free will is also thoroughly vetted in both the Old and New Testaments. Joshua 24:15 says "as for me and my house we will serve the Lord." Deuteronomy 30:19 says, "I have set before you life and death, blessings and curses, therefore choose life." In 2 Peter 2:3–9, the Lord says that he is not willing that any should perish but that all should come to repentance. These verses appear to be "free will" statements supporting the idea that our eternal fate rests within ourselves. So let's investigate whether there is a bridge between these two great church dogmas. In an examination of God's precepts, we know he is omniscient (all-knowing), a trait that encompasses his ability to "foresee" all future events. God had the ability to see every human life before the Earth was created. He, therefore, had the foreknowledge to know every name that would be written in the Book of Life (Revelation 20:15). The names of the "saved" in the Book of Life were known by God through his foreknowledge. This is not an example of God predetermining their fates, it is an example of God foreknowing their free will choices. Visualize, if you will, a lottery cage spinning around with fifty numbered balls inside. Each time the button is pushed, a single ball, through absolute

Are We Predestined to Heaven or Hell? (Continued)

randomness, is perfectly positioned by the selection port and is siphoned out. Once six balls have been randomly selected, you may see the winning numbers, the "elect" spoken of in scripture. Even before the cage began to spin, God foreknew what six winning numbers would be selected. God did not reach into the spinning cage and select the winning numbers (predestination). The winning numbers were selected randomly (through free will). Obviously, this analogy is not meant to be anything more than a simple mechanism to illustrate a very complex doctrine. We know that God's will is immutable; therefore, his will is always accomplished. We also know that God's antecedent will (existing before time) is for all to be saved (2 Peter 3:9). Unfortunately, through the exercise of their own free will, some people choose to reject God's antecedent will. This rejection of God's plan for salvation will trigger God's consequential will, and that soul will face judgment outside the saving grace of Christ.

The Big Bang Theory

Christians are sometimes called upon by the secular community to explain their position on the creation of the universe and other natural phenomenon. With the emergence of the big bang theory in the 1970's and its universal acceptance by 1990, the scientific community has coalesced around a time frame for the existence of the universe of about fourteen billion years. This is where Christians face a conundrum. Do they believe the scientific projections, or do they believe, as verbatim, the creation story told in Genesis chapter one. If taken as verbatim, the Genesis "six-day" creation sequence places the age of the Earth at approximately six thousand years. This time frame is calculated by an examination of the unbroken listings of genealogies provided in scripture from Adam to Jesus. Most people given the opportunity to travel and witness the incredible effects of nature, such as the awe-inspiring Grand Canyon, will simply scoff at the idea of an Earth being only six thousand years old. This debate within Christian circles should not predispose one's thinking out of loyalty to a specific dogma but, instead, to keep an open mind as to what Moses intended in writing the first chapter of Genesis. 2 Timothy 3:16 says that all scripture is given by inspiration of God and is profitable for doctrine, for reproof, for correction, and for instruction in righteousness. 2 Peter 1:21 says, "for the prophesy came not at any time by the will of man, but holy men of God spoke as they were moved by the Holy Spirit." These scriptures clearly articulate that the Bible is the inspired Word of God, whose chapters and verses were set into writing under the guidance of the Holy Spirit. Therefore, the veracity of the book of Genesis is not in question here, only it's interpretation. In examining the first chapter, the phrase "evening and morning" is often used to conclude a definitive act of creation. A typical period of evening and morning is approximately twenty-four hours, governed by one rotation of the Earth. Therefore, evening and morning are the result of either facing toward the sun (morning), or away from the sun (evening), as the Earth rotates on its axis. This transition from light to dark was made beautifully visual through the cameras of our astronauts while they orbited around the Earth in the early 1960's. With each quick eighty-minute orbit, the astronauts were able to experience a sunrise and sunset all within approximately one hour. For the astronaut, an "evening and morning" was not a twenty-four-hour cycle (Earth's perspective) but eighty minutes (space perspective). From God's perspective, "a day is like a thousand years and a thousand years as a day" (Peter 3:8). As scientific methodologies have advanced over the last century, and especially in the field of computing technology, scientists have been able to reach far out into space to unravel the mysteries of the universe. The terms "space and time" become intertwined within the warping effects of huge gravitational fields such as "black holes." Time can be speeded up or slowed down depending on gravitational forces. Advancements in optical technology have allowed telescopes such as the Hubble to view galaxies at distances from the Earth that are incomprehensible. Most Christians believe in science and do not refute the findings of astronomy or geology, yet they find themselves boxed in with what to actually believe about the Biblical record of creation. The question before us is simple. Was the book of Genesis written to present a literal account of God's act of creation? Here are a few things to consider. The word chosen by Moses to represent "day" in the Hebrew dialect is "yom." Early Hebrew has five meanings for "yom," all being related to time. It may be used to represent a typical twenty-four-hour period, or "yom" may be used to represent a great expanse of time. The use of the word "yom" may actually represent vast creative "epochs" each taking millions, even billions of years. The words "evening and morning," which Moses

The Big Bang Theory (Continued)

selected as termination phrases for each act of creation, appear to be in reverse order. If interpreted literally, did the creative acts occur in the hours of darkness? These ambiguities in word selection and sequencing in the Genesis account, when coupled with the fact that we don't know what Moses really meant to convey when using the word "yom," supports a credible opinion that the Genesis record was written as a metaphorical interpretation of God's creative act. This discussion is not intended to present a stumbling block to anyone's knowledge or faith, but John 8:33 says, "If you know the truth, the truth shall set you free." As Christians, we stand in truth that God created all things. Spiritual equilibrium comes from the freedom we are given to observe the creative works of God without condemnation.

Kicking Against the Goads

In ancient times, farmers often used a wooden staff with a sharpened point to direct their oxen when pulling carts. This stick was called a "goad." Oxen were well-suited to the task of pulling but tended to be stubborn in nature, thus requiring a gentle prod with the farmer's goad to walk in a straight path. Sometimes an ox would rebel against this gentle prod by kicking backward against the goad, causing the sharp point of the staff to stab into their hide. This was painful to the ox, as one would expect, but it was the direct result of the ox's stubbornness in not wanting to be obedient to the farmer's direction. It is of interest to note that Christ used this particular analogy when referring to Saul's behavior on the road to Damascus in Acts 9:5. I have often wondered why our Lord chose to use this unusual phrase, "kicking against the goads," as it didn't seem to fit the dynamics of the moment. We know from scripture that Saul was on his way to Damascus to persecute Christians. God chose this moment to intervene in his life in a spectacular way. Saul was struck down by the light and glory of God, and as he lay on the ground, Jesus called to him saying, "Saul, Saul, why do you persecute me. It is hard for thee to kick against the goads." Up to this moment, Saul had been a proud enforcer of Jewish law. As a member of the Pharisee sect and a Roman citizen, Saul carried great respect among the people. He was utterly convinced that his duty lay in ferreting out the scattered pockets of Christians, whom he considered to be a cult of blasphemers and stoning them to death in accordance with Jewish law. However, in God's eyes, Saul was acting like a stubborn willful ox, determined to go his own way. I'm sure that the Lord had prodded Saul many times with his "goad" trying to soften his heart and turn him away from this path of destruction, but Saul was stubborn. Because of his resistance to the "prods," God had to up the ante, so to speak, by knocking him down in the road and making him blind. Saul wisely submitted his will to Jesus. This incident with Saul illustrates the mechanism by which the Holy Spirit works within each of us. Our lives are continuously guided by the gentle prods of the Spirit, making our consciences aware of sinful behavior and the absolute need to receive the cleansing Grace so freely given by our Lord Jesus. But we are often a stiff-necked and stubborn people, willfully kicking against the "goad" and refusing to follow the direction of God. With each kick, we hurt ourselves and grieve the Holy Spirit. Each "kick" represents misdirected willfulness on our part, resulting in the need for additional training from the goad of God. May our prayer always be to hear and joyfully receive the mild chastening of the Lord, "for whom the Lord loveth, He chasteneth" (Hebrews 12:6).

The Mystery of God

There are a number of mysteries in God's creative work that we are not given to comprehend. The concept of eternity, for example, is one that most people find difficult to gather their minds around. We may experience the "sensation" of eternity whenever we point our finger up to a constellation in the night sky. Just off the tip of our extended finger, we see an endless universe filled with billions of stars and galaxies so far away that it becomes unfathomable to our minds (there just has to be an end to the universe). We accept our scientific observations because our eyes and our senses reflect that truth, but the idea of endless space, i.e., eternity, remains elusive to our minds. As temporal beings, we associate everything in our lives with time. We are born into this life, and at some point, we will die. We drive our cars from here to there. We start careers when we're young and retire from them when we're old. These are familiar experiences we all share in a world dictated by time. Eternity, however, is a dimension not governed by time. Earthbound constraints simply do not apply to the endless reaches of the universe, or to the nature of God. As Christians, we have confidence in our eternal destination through assurances found in scripture, but not all theological questions can be answered so easily. There is much debate over our soul's journey following death. Do our spirits instantly transit to heaven, or do we "sleep" in the grave until the voice of our Lord stirs our consciousness to life? The answers to these questions, and many others, fall within the secrets of God, which are restricted from our present understanding (Deuteronomy 29:29). Try as we might, we will never fully understand these hidden truths. Another of God's mysteries centers around the many names for him found in the Bible. In Revelation 1:8, God is identified as "the Alpha and the Omega," the first and last letters in the Greek alphabet. In Genesis 3:14, God provides his name to Moses as "I am that I am" (Yahweh). In Psalm 90:3, God is described as "everlasting and eternal" by the name "El Olam." These scriptures, and numerous others, provide the believer with insight into God's true eternal nature. He has no beginning in time and no ending. In the infinite expanse of his eternal being, God chose to create the dimension of time for his purpose. Within this "window" in eternity, God ordained all the events documented in the Bible from Genesis to Revelation. Creating finite from infinite, flesh and blood from spirit, God proclaimed that it was "very good" (Genesis 1:31). This "window of time" has existed for at least six thousand years, or, depending on how one interprets Genesis chapter one, it may have existed for as long as fifteen billion years, but at some point in the future, according to scripture, God will close off this dimension of time, and all things will once again return to their eternal state. We do not know the hour or the day of this transformation, but we know through scripture that it is coming. Our time on this Earth is as a "vapor," here today and gone tomorrow (James 4:14). The finality of death completes our experience in this dimension of "time" and ushers our soul into eternity, where all earthbound hindrances will be removed before the full glory of our eternal God.

Spiritual Peace

What is spiritual peace? John 16:33 says, "These things I have spoken to you, that in me ye might have peace. In the world ye shall have tribulation, but take courage, I have overcome the world." God is first addressed as Jehovah Shalom (the Lord is peace) in the Book of Judges 6:24 by Gideon. It was during a time of spiritual drought among the Israelites, which had led to their enslavement by the Midianites. The people were filled with a spirit of fear and depression. The Lord instructed Gideon to lead his people out of servitude and return to a life of peace through God. If we wish to fully understand the essence of spiritual peace, we must first examine the drivers of anxiety in our lives. A troubled spirit is often characterized by excessive worry, fear, disquietude, depression, helplessness, and hopelessness. The primary generators of this mental unrest change over time. In our youth, these factors generally revolve around relationships, disharmony in one's family, educational challenges, or employment circumstances. Later in life, anxiety and restlessness relate more to worries we have on personal health issues, financial concerns, or marital/family conflict. These feelings of unrest may also be related to the inner workings of the Holy Spirit, as he convicts us of sin. According to statistics, forty million Americans seek treatment at some point in their lives, for symptoms of anxiety or depression. Even Jesus suffered in the agony of despair as he prayed in the Garden of Gethsemane (Matthew 26:37–38). As with all the fruits of the Spirit described in the fifth chapter of Galatians, spiritual *peace* is acquired through a progressive faith-based process of sanctification. We each desire to attain a lasting spiritual peace, a peace that can stand true in the throes of upheaval and sorrow, a peace where we can truly say that "all things work together for good to them that love God, to them who are the called according to His purpose" (Romans 8:28). This scripture doesn't say all things *are* good. It says all things *work together* for good. Getting a diagnosis of cancer is not a "good" thing, but when it works together with everything else that God uses from that experience, it will produce a good thing. It is in such times of trial where the fruit of the Spirit, "peace," becomes a soothing balm to the Christian. No matter what our circumstances are, we know that God is still on his throne (Psalm 47:8), and nothing can separate the believer from the love of God through Christ Jesus (Romans 8:39). Christians who manifest this level of peace in their lives have attained a level of spiritual "reality" where there is no place for apprehension, or sudden fear, or the workings of evil. Their confidence is continually in the Lord (Proverbs 3:24–26). This kind of peace is Spirit-filled. The secular world yearns for this same type of peace, but the Bible says they cannot attain it. Isaiah 57:19 says that only God can bring lasting peace and healing. The 23rd psalm is oft quoted, even in the secular world, for its timeless message of peace and restorative qualities. King David, the psalmist, uses a compelling vocabulary in describing God's deliberate hand in providing shelter for his people in times of worry. Phrases such as "The Lord maketh me lie down in green pastures," "He leadeth me beside still waters," and "He restoreth my soul" are not passive prose. They ring with power! To the Christian who is tormented with grief, stress, fear, or sleeplessness over worry, God promises that he will bring you out of despair and will restore your sleep (Proverbs 3:24–26). We often block this gift of peace through our own stubbornness, creating unnecessary turmoil in our lives. It is then that God must place his calming hand upon us. That is his solemn promise to all of us if we allow his intervention in our lives. I have felt that calming hand on my persecuted soul many times in my life. Glory be to God.

Pathways to Prayer

Prayer is our pathway to our Creator, and it is a deeply personal experience. Although Jesus provided a general framework of prayer in Matthew 6:9, our individual approach to God's mercy seat is as different among believers, as is our ideologies. In Matthew 6:9, we are instructed that prayer be expressed to our heavenly Father, first in worship and thanksgiving and then in making requests (Psalm 107:8). As we pray to our heavenly Father, Jesus presents us with great joy, as righteous beings, cleansed of all sin through his atonement (Jude 1:24–25, John 14:6). The Holy Spirit also intercedes for us when we do not know how to pray effectively (Romans 8:26). God desires this intimate communion with man, and it is pleasing to him (Proverbs 15:8). Through the cleansing power of Christ's redemption, we are made righteous, our Adamic relationship is restored, and we can once again walk in the cool of the day in Eden with our Creator (Genesis 3:8). In the body of Christ (believers), there are those among us who have been gifted with a prayer diligence beyond the norm. Intercessory prayer is not specifically named as gift of the Spirit (Romans 12:6) but is identified in many scriptures (Colossians 4:12, Acts 12:5, and 1 Corinthians 4:12), as a vital component within the body of Christ. These, "prayer warriors" or "intercessors," have been blessed with a strength to stay focused on specific prayer needs. Through the power of the Holy Spirit, they maintain a prayer channel of uninterrupted intercession that is less susceptible to the interference and noise of their daily lives. For the rest of us who have the "noise" issue when we pray, we can seek solace in the knowledge that the Spirit of God searches our hearts and lifts up our feeble attempts with the power of his intercession for us (Romans 8:26). To be true prayer warriors, the "reality" of God and his gift of Jesus must be upon us. Oswald Chambers speaks of the immense importance of keeping the "reality of the redemption" foremost in our hearts. We are all guilty of allowing our relationship with God to be less "real" at times. In scripture, there is a parallel between our relationship with God and our relationship with our husbands or wives. We are the bride of Christ. The love and adoration we felt for our wife or husband on our wedding day is the same feeling God desires for our relationship to him. Unfortunately, as with our earthly relationships, our passions for our Savior, that pure adoration we felt at our redemption, may become dulled. I often think of the grief we must bring the Holy Spirit each day with our stubbornness and willfulness. There is a scene in the movie *Cool Hand Luke*, where Paul Newman, being chased after escaping from prison, finds himself in a dark deserted church. He gazes up at the ceiling rafters and asks God for help. After several minutes with no response from the silent rafters above, Newman responds by saying, "Well, I wouldn't answer either if I were you." Unfortunately, that is how the majority of the world thinks of prayer. Something to do when calamity strikes and then when we get no immediate response, assume that there is no God, or if there is, he is uncaring and unresponsive. 2 Chronicles 7:14 says, "If my people, who are called by my Name, shall humble themselves, and pray, and seek my Face, and turn from their wicked ways, then will I hear from Heaven and will forgive their sin, and will heal their land." As we enter into his presence in prayer, may we confess our transgressions, admit our weaknesses, be washed clean and sanctified in Christ's blood, and then come boldly before the mercy seat of God. When we do these things, we can be assured that our Heavenly Father hears our prayers and is ever merciful to us. To him be the glory.

Prayer Warrior

I will be the first to admit that I am not an eloquent prayer warrior. I don't like to pray in public, or in front of other people, because I have a tendency to focus on how I'm sounding and not on my conversation with God. Apostle Paul tells us in 1 Thessalonians 5:16–18 to rejoice always, pray without ceasing, and in everything, give thanks, for this is the will of God in Jesus Christ. Whenever I need a spiritual standard, I try to look to the words of Jesus in the Gospels. In Matthew 6:5–8, our Lord gives specific examples of what to avoid when praying. In verses 9–13, Jesus provides us with a general prayer format. These passages in Matthew were not intended to place restrictions on our prayer life. Their purpose is to instruct us on how to pray effectively. Praying in public while beating our chests and calling attention to ourselves was the Pharisee method, and Jesus despised that behavior. Praying in a public setting should be done carefully, with a sincere heart, and never for our own edification. In the Bible there are many scriptures which provide instruction on how we should present our requests before God. The Lord desires our communion, just as an earthly father desires the love and adoration of his children (Matthew 7:9–11). As Christians, we sometimes misunderstand this unique relationship with a loving God, who, on one hand, desires to give us the pleasures of our heart, but on the other hand, must align these requests within his sovereign will. Here lies a conundrum. If we pray for financial help, or for a specific healing, we are petitioning God to intervene in a positive way. If we do not receive this, scripture instructs us to continue to "knock" on the prayer door (Matthew 7:7). As we continue to pray, we are fervent, righteous, and focused in our prayer endeavors in accordance with James 5:16 but may still receive no relief to the problem. We begin to wonder at this point why God is not responding, why he is seemingly silent to our situation. We rarely feel that God may have already answered our prayer with a "no." Why do we feel this uncertainty? As earthly fathers, we always filter our own children's requests through a checklist of what's good for them. We may answer our children's requests with a "no" when we perceive their submissions are not to their benefit. In like manner, our heavenly Father evaluates our requests in accordance with his will. Hebrews 13:21 tells us that our life has one primary purpose and that is to further the glory of God through Christ. That is the will of God. 1 John 5:14 says that if we ask anything "according to his will," he hears us. The caveat is that we can't always know what the will of God is for a particular circumstance when we make our prayer. 1 Peter 4:19 says, "Wherefore, let them that suffer according to the will of God commit the keeping of their souls to him in well-doing, as unto a faithful Creator." This scripture, along with Apostle Paul's experience in 2 Corinthians 12:9, demonstrates that there are circumstances where difficult circumstances may actually be in the will of God for us. The Apostle Paul, as I have previously mentioned, prayed on three different occasions to be healed of some "thorn in his flesh," which may have been vision related (Galatians 4:15). Paul did not receive relief from this "thorn" because it was not in God's will to do so. At the time Paul prayed for healing, he was not privy to God's greater purpose for his affliction. God used the example of Paul's denied prayer request to teach a spiritual lesson to the body of Christ. Simply put, "we don't always get what we want." Sometimes the answer we receive is "no," even for someone as influential as Paul. If we are living in obedience, growing in the fruits of the Spirit, and placing Christ first, our prayer requests will reflect this position of "not my will, but thine be done." The Holy Spirit, searching our hearts and knowing the mind of our Father, will intercede for us accordingly.

The Concept of Eternal Security

There has been a lot of discussion in theological circles over eternal security. If a Christian (definition being that at some point in their lives they accepted Jesus as Savior) falls away from Christ, makes a willful decision to become a nonbeliever, and dies in that unbelief, will God still grant that person eternal life in heaven? Historically, there have been two main avenues of thought on this issue. The Calvinistic approach, named after John Calvin, the famous French theologian, is accepted by most of the Protestant churches and adheres to an ideology called the "Perseverance of the Saints," or more commonly referred to as "once saved, always saved." The other ideology is called Arminianism, named after Jacobus Arminius, a Dutch theologian, who, in 1614, proscribed that Christians, through their free will, can lose their eternal salvation by renouncing Christ. These two differing theological dogmas have scriptures which are important to their point of view. Calvin's doctrine is severely challenged by several scriptural passages in Hebrews 6:4–6 and Hebrews 10:26–29. These scriptural passages seem to reflect a significant risk to the eternal salvation of Christians who willingly resist the sanctification process of the Holy Spirit and return to a state of apostasy. The "unforgivable sin," referred to by Jesus in Matthew 12:31–31, speaks of blasphemy against the Holy Spirit. If a person turns away from the cross and enters back into a life of apostasy, he has created a blasphemous rebuke to the assistance and guidance of the Holy Spirit. In Hebrews 6:6, it speaks to the fact that such a person cannot be granted repentance a second time, for such would represent a second crucifixion of Christ. This constitutes the "unforgivable sin," for which there is no longer an avenue open for redemption. I do not believe this scripture is referring to the occasional "backsliding" or carnality that may sometimes creep into a Christian's life from time to time. The loss of redemption described in Matthew 12:31 would be the result of a willful and permanent decision by the person to enter back into a reprobate state from whence he came, such as found in Revelation 14:9–1, where people choose to take the mark of the Beast and worship Satan. This willful decision will result in salvation lost for these people. The Calvinist defense to this argument is formulated around the definition of "salvation." The parable of the sower (Matthew 13:1–23), who casts seeds on rocky ground, is often given as an example of someone who hears the Word, and may even present a repentant outward appearance, but whose heart was never in total acceptance of Christ. This example, they feel, meets the Hebrews 6 criteria of tasting the heavenly manna but not willing to commit heart, soul, and spirit to the Lord. Another example can be found in Matthew 19:16 where the rich young man approached Jesus asking what he could do to attain eternal life. He had lived a religious life trying to be obedient to the Commandments but was unwilling to sell his possessions and follow Christ. Calvinists would proclaim that these are examples of people who appeared to be Christians but had never actually received eternal salvation in the first place. By expanding the once-saved-always-saved ideology, any Christian who falls away from Christ would represent a *false* salvation experience (rocky soil). It certainly reinforces the idea that each one of us needs to examine our own salvation with fear and trembling (Philippians 2:12). Another conundrum to this eternal security debate would be the thousands of "new converts" at a Billy Graham crusade. At the altar call, each of these people "feel" the conviction in their hearts and go forward of their own free will. They pray the prayer of salvation, asking forgiveness of their sins and receiving Jesus into their hearts. Most, I'm sure, come away from the experience feeling that they have received salvation, but many fall away over the weeks and months that follow. Calvinists will argue that that the "sower parable" covers this phenomenon, i.e.,

The Concept of Eternal Security (Continued)

those people who turn away over time were never saved in the first place. I would argue that the Billy Graham "converts" on that night would disagree with that assumption. Free will is one of the great cornerstones of God's eternal plan, and through it, we either accept God's grace through Jesus Christ, or reject him. We know from John 3:16 that it is God's desire that everyone should receive salvation through his Son. We also know that many who appear to be Christians will reject Christ and the path to salvation he represents. The debate over eternal security refers only to those souls. John Calvin believed that once a Christian came under the umbrella of grace, their free will and choice disappeared (once saved, always saved). Jacobus Arminius believed that a "saved" person retains this personal freedom to make choices, even to the point of rejecting Christ at a later time. Scriptural evidence may be found in support of both points of view. It is the responsibility of every Christian to search their own hearts for evidence of the in-dwelling Holy Spirit, who is not only the arbiter of our prayers before God, but is the discerner of our thoughts and intents (Hebrews 4:12).

The Twenty-third Psalm

I have always loved the 23rd psalm. David wrote this psalm over three thousand years ago when he was the King of Israel. I'm sure as he began to write, his mind drifted back to a simpler time, when his sole governance consisted only of a flock of sheep. As a boy, David learned the skills of guiding and protecting the flocks of sheep entrusted to him by his father. It required a firm but loving hand to keep his flocks in order. The first several verses of the twenty-third psalm seem to reflect his youthful association with his sheep. David knew that a good shepherd makes sure that the physical and emotional needs of his sheep are cared for. Just as in humans, sheep undergo stress when confronted with fearful experiences. It is the shepherd's responsibility to reduce or eliminate any harmful factors in the environment that might create panic or restlessness within the flock. David could well remember the time when he had to kill, single-handedly, a bear and a lion that had taken a lamb (1 Samuel 17:35). He begins the psalm with an acknowledgment that God is our loving shepherd. We are his sheep, his people, and his flock. With that simple introduction, King David set the tone for the words to follow. Just as the Israelites were given the fiery pillar of God to follow toward their promised land (Exodus 13:21), David was guided by the Holy Spirit to write the words which would serve as a healing balm for all believers. Probably no other passage has had such far-reaching effects on troubled souls as the 23rd psalm. There is a wonderful peace that moves within the words and reverberates again and again from the first verse to the last. This is a psalm written for God's people. It is a pure love note from our heavenly Father. The Lord "maketh" me to lie down in green pastures, the Lord "leadeth" me beside the still waters, and he "restoreth" my soul. These passages are uplifting for the weary, the downtrodden of spirit. The words "maketh, leadeth, and restoreth" ring with power as God intervenes in our lives. "He leadeth me in the path of righteousness for His name's sake," a passage revealing the active role the Holy Spirit takes in every Christian's life. "Yea though I walk through the valley of the shadow of death, I will fear no evil, for thou art with me." One of the most quoted verses of the Bible, even by people who profess no religious affiliation. This verse has provided comfort and peace to untold millions of people facing serious health issues or fear in their environment. "Thy rod and thy staff, they comfort me." As a physical symbol of Moses's authority and as the protecting staff of a loving shepherd, the rod and staff has guided Christians by the gentle touch of the "goad" of God. "Thou prepareth a table before me in the presence of mine enemies, thou anointeth my head with oil, my cup runneth over." As Christians, we know that our heavenly Father ministers to our needs just as an earthly father and mother care for their own children. We receive the blessing of peace through these nurturing verses, knowing we are God's chosen people, protected in the shadow of his wings. "Surely goodness and mercy shall follow me all the days of my life, and I will dwell in the house of the Lord forever." This passage provides tremendous reassurance for all Christians. It doesn't guarantee a certain length of life, just a Spirit-filled life of peace and joy, regardless of one's circumstances. The greatest blessing of all comes at the endcap of this psalm, where we are promised to forever live in the house of the Lord. As was oft quoted by a former pastor of mine, now passed on, "All this and heaven too." Some Christians in this life have burdens, which seem far more daunting than others. I do believe that God pours out a greater portion of his peace to those who have these additional issues. I certainly witnessed this additional anointing in the life of my earthly father, who, though wheelchair-bound for life, rejoiced every day in God's mercy and love. Thank you, heavenly Father, for the gift of love found the shepherd's psalm.

The Tribulation Controversy

Christians are a forward-looking people. We are looking forward to Christ's glorious return to Earth. In Matthew 24:42, the Lord instructs us to be ever vigilant for the signs of his 2nd coming. The date for this event is not found in scripture. In fact, Jesus says in Matthew 24:36 that the exact date is known only to the Father, but regardless of that fact, we are still instructed by Christ to be watchful for the events leading up to his return. Jesus begins this discussion of the end-time in Matthew 24:2 as he takes his disciples to the Mount of Olives to show them the buildings of the existing temple. In verse 2, he declares that this temple will be completely destroyed (which it was in 70 AD), thus prompting the disciples to inquire further about these future events. Jesus provides them with a detailed description of the end-time in Matthew chapter 24, culminating in his triumphant 2nd coming. Daniel the prophet, writing six hundred years before Christ, had, in mathematical clarity, laid out the exact same timetable for this final period on Earth. Daniel used a seventy-week calendar with the last week detailing the Tribulation. Each week represents seven years, so each day is one year. A little confusing at first, but it becomes quite clear in the later chapters of Daniel, where, in his prophetic vision, he spoke in a concise manner about the Tribulation period. The accuracy of Daniel's prophesy was confirmed by Jesus in Matthew 24:15. The Great Tribulation period of seven years will be divided exactly in half by world events. The beginning of this seven-year period appears to start with the signing of a significant peace treaty between Israel and other nations, probably brokered by the new world leader alluded to in Daniel 9:27 and 1 Thessalonians 5:3. During these first three-and-a-half years following the peace treaty, there will be ever-increasing cataclysmic events involving wars, famines, earthquakes, and disease outbreaks. Human depravity explodes during these first years of the Tribulation as God removes the restraining effects of the Holy Spirit (2 Thessalonians 2:7). This initial three-year time period is also characterized by flagrant discrimination and violence toward Christians. The last three-and-a-half years of the Tribulation become far worse, as graphically described by Jesus in Matthew 24:15–22. This last period is heralded by a singular and world-shattering act of blasphemy (Revelation 13:6) by the world leader. The Antichrist stands in the "holy place" (Jerusalem), abolishes all Jewish customs and religious ceremonies (Daniel 9:27), and essentially declares himself God (2 Thessalonians 2:5). This single vile act by this satanic world leader will usher in the final three-and-a-half years of the Tribulation, years, which are so violent and cataclysmic that God must intervene in the end to save the lives of new believers (Matthew 24:22). The seven years of the Great Tribulation are finally brought to a close when the Lord Jesus returns to Earth in great glory (Matthew 24:27–31), surrounded by a host of saints (pre-raptured Christians). The great battle of Armageddon is fought (Revelation 17:16) against the armies of the Antichrist, which are defeated and cast into the lake of fire (Revelation 19:19–20). Christ ascends to his rightful authority as King of kings in Jerusalem, followed by one thousand years of millennial reign on Earth (Revelation 20:6–7). Post-millennial events on Earth will be discussed in later *Musings*.

The Rapture

Any discussion about the "end-time" events must include the subject of the "rapture" of Christ's church. Most Christian church denominations accept the scriptural premise that there will be a period of Great Tribulation prior to Christ's victorious return to Earth. The question presented is whether believers (the bride of Christ) will have to endure these bad times, or will they be translated (like Enoch of the OT) to heaven prior to the seven years described by the book of Daniel in chapter 9. The most commonly held belief by Christians is set forth so beautifully in 1 Thessalonians 4:13–18. In this passage, Christians, both living and dead, will be called up to heaven by Jesus, who meets them in the clouds with great joy. The exact placement of this event in relation to the Tribulation period is the subject of this debate. Our focus will be on the three most widely excepted dogmas identified by their prefixes, pre-, mid-, and post-Tribulation. As the prefixes indicate, the tenets of each is postulated on the timing of the event as it occurs in relation to the seven-year period of the Antichrist. Pre-Tribulation believers use scriptures, such as Luke 21:36, Revelation 3:10, and 1 Thessalonians 1:10, to promote their position of the rapture occurring before the Tribulation period begins. Mid-Tribulation believers use scriptures such as Daniel 7:25, where it seems to indicate a "wearing out of the saints" by the Antichrist for three-and-a-half years, hence, mid-Tribulation. Post-Tribulation loyalists believe that all end-time scriptures, such as Matthew 24 and Revelation 19, are describing Christ's second coming only, and therefore, the "rapture" will occur at the end of the seven-year-tribulation period when Christ returns. As with many theological issues, the rapture debate has a lengthy eschatological history associated with it, as differing opinions by religious scholars have been forthcoming over centuries. The word "'rapture" is not actually used by the Apostle Paul in 1 Thessalonians 4:17. Paul used the Greek word "harpazo," which translates as "caught up, or taken away." Luke 21:36 says, "Watch ye therefore, and pray always, that he may be accounted worthy to escape all these things that are to come to pass and to stand before the Son of man." Revelation 3:10 says, "Because thou has kept the word of my patience, I also will keep thee from the hour of temptation which shall come upon all the world, to try them that dwell on the earth." These scriptures seem to speak to the removal of believers before the Tribulation troubles begin. As Jesus talks directly to his disciples in Matthew 24:29–31, he is addressing the period of time at the end of the Tribulation (verse 29), and it is clear in verse 30 that he is describing his triumphant return to Earth. It is verse 31 that holds a key to our "rapture" discussion. Jesus clearly says that he will send his angels to gather the elect (believers) from the four winds, from one end of heaven to the other. It would appear from that one verse that the bride of Christ is not only residing in heaven but widely scattered throughout, which points to a "rapture" event having already occurred at an earlier point, either mid- or pre-Tribulation. As believers in Christ, we have much to look forward to. If we die before these future events take place, we are assured of waking to the voice of our Lord calling us to glory. If we are yet alive when this happens, we will experience what Enoch and Elijah felt as the Lord whisked them up to heaven. It is my opinion that our merciful and loving Father will not subject his church to the awful experiences of the Tribulation, and we will, in the twinkling of an eye (1 Corinthians 15:52), be transformed into his glorious image. Amen.

End-Time Sequence of Events

Rapture of all Christians living and dead to heaven (1 Thessalonians 4:12)

Start of seven years of tribulation with the last three-and-a-half years being the worst (Daniel 11:11)

Christ's second coming with all the saints and angels (Revelation 19:11–16, Matthew 24:29-31)

Battle of Armageddon: Antichrist and false prophet thrown into hell; Satan chained for one thousand years (Revelation 19:11–20)

Christ's millennial reign on Earth (one thousand years); Christians in "glorified bodies" are part of this earthly reign (Revelation 20:4–7)

Satan unchained at the end of the thousand-year millennial reign, raises an evil army, and is destroyed by Christ (Revelation 20:7)

Satan is finally cast into hell for all eternity (Revelation 20:11)

Jesus resurrects all the unsaved dead and presides over the great white judgment throne (Revelation 20:11–13)

The unsaved, after judgment, are cast into the lake of fire for varying periods of punishment (Revelation 20:15)

After their punishment time is served, God, in his mercy, will annihilate their souls for all eternity (Annihilation Theory)

God creates a new heaven and a new Earth with a new city of Jerusalem (Revelation 21:1–2)

Christians live and reign with Jesus for all eternity (Revelation 22:5)

Sanctification

As I write in *Musings*, I am reminded of the Apostle Paul's admonition in 2 Timothy 2:14–18, "Do not engage in vain babblings or words of no profit." Paul, who himself often participated in spiritual debates with the Greeks and Romans, warns us to not argue over points of scripture which are not necessary for the sanctification of the individual. So let's talk about what sanctification means. Once a soul is saved through grace, the arduous task of living a godly life begins. We know through John 12:31 that the world we live in is under the domination of Satan, and as Christians, we are to "resist the Devil" (James 4:7). While this appears easy on face value, it is agonizingly difficult in real time. The Apostle Paul himself lamented over his own lack of self-control when, in Romans 7:24, he cried out, "Oh wretched man that I am." Because of this difficulty, a large part of Paul's writings in the New Testament are devoted to correcting the miscues made by new believers. At the time when Paul wrote the Epistles, he was the premier ambassador for Christ in all of Asia Minor, where most of the non-Jewish population (gentiles) worshipped Greek and Roman idols. As the number of new converts to Christ grew through his Holy Spirit-inspired preaching, Paul frequently found himself in the undesirable position of having to "shepherd" his new flocks. This was not a position in which Paul wished to be, as he saw his primary calling to be evangelism. But Paul recognized the seriousness of the situation and his responsibility through the Holy Spirit—to rectify the mistakes and false teachings which were cropping up among his churches in Asia Minor. He addressed these issues through letters, which he dictated to specific churches, and which, when hand delivered, would be read to the targeted congregations. The majority of the Pauline letters in the New

Testament are written with an endeavor to instruct, inspire, and at times, admonish members of his new churches according to their behaviors. This newfound freedom in Christ presented significant challenges to the Jewish status quo, especially in areas of dietary law, circumcision, and behavior toward gentile believers. Paul's ability to negotiate these testy doctrinal waters without alienating new Jewish Christians, or their worldly Gentile counterparts, was crucial for the early church. Through the instruction provided in Paul's letters, every Christian is given the tools for leading a holy life. All sanctification begins with salvation, and on that premise, most Christians agree. Christ provides atonement for all the sins of our former life, and we are washed clean at that moment. Keeping that righteousness over the course of one's lifetime, however, requires spiritual discipline and commitment (Romans 6:1). We are instructed in Romans 6:12 to bring into subjection our former sinful habits of the old life and embrace the "new man" under Christ, where we do not allow sin to reign in our mortal bodies. Thus begins the journey along the path of righteousness in all aspects of our lives. When Paul said, "Let not sin reign," he is speaking directly to Christians, people who have already received initial sanctification through Christ's atoning grace but face the daily battle over temptations of the flesh in a world dominated by Satan. Sin is the obvious obstruction along the path of righteousness. Sin is anything that violates God's law, vis-à-vis, the two great commandments given to us by Jesus in Matthew 22:37–40. "Love God with all our heart, soul and spirit, and love our fellow man as we love ourselves." These two commandments incorporate all of our thoughts, words, and deeds. By simply not loving God with all our heart, or by not helping our fellow man as we help ourselves, we fall under the sin of omission. This commandment requires total commitment. Something as small as wearing a WWJD bracelet can be instrumental in promoting daily awareness of our relationship to God and man.

Sanctification (Continued)

Anything that helps to remind us daily of the need for sanctification (putting on the new man) is a good thing. How often can one say they've not committed the sin of omission concerning their love for the Lord? We all come short of living a purely righteous life. When we receive salvation, the Lord forgives all of our sins ("positional forgiveness"), and we are made spotless before the throne of God through the blood of Jesus. But unfortunately, as we go forward as Christians, we will continue to sin occasionally (frequently), and if we leave this sin unacknowledged, it will grieve the Holy Spirit (Ephesians 4:30), restricting his work in our lives. Much like unchecked levels of cholesterol in our bodies, willful sin leads to a buildup of spiritual plaque. The Apostle Paul recognized "carnality" as an inherent danger to a life of spiritual righteousness and worked tirelessly to caution believers against indulging in the "works of the flesh" (Galatians 5:19). The result of unrepentant sin in our lives is analogous to the strained relationship between a father and a child caused by disobedience. That relationship does not improve until the source of the disobedience ends. Our repentance of daily sin (relational forgiveness) and our commitment to refrain from "works of the flesh" restores us to the "good graces" of the Lord and is pleasing to the Holy Spirit.

Communion with God

How often throughout the day do we talk with God? Do we pursue him earnestly as Enoch of the Old Testament did, or do we confine ourselves to the occasional spiritual thought? We are unique in all of creation in that we were made in God's "image and likeness" (Genesis 1:26). Unlike the angels, our habitat is earthbound, where we see through a glass darkly (1 Corinthians 13:12). Our senses are denied the light and majesty of God's heavenly throne. Thus, we find ourselves "a little lower than the angels" (Hebrews 2:7–9) until that moment when the Rapture will release our spirit into the eternal realm of God. Adam was created perfect, in a perfect world, until sin removed Adam's righteous state, placing a "veil" between God and man until the coming of Christ, the "Lamb of God who took away the sins of the world" (John 1:29). The cross restored the original Adamic relationship by tearing open the veil in the Holy of Holies, allowing, once more, the pure unrestricted access to almighty God (Matthew 27:51). No more do we need a priest to intercede for us other than the high priest Jesus Christ. Since the time of King Solomon, this thick Temple curtain had but one purpose—to separate a Holy God from a sinful people. Although often overlooked and overshadowed by the enormity of the cross and Christ's resurrection, the tearing of the Temple veil was probably the most significant symbolic event of the atonement. For the first time in over four thousand years, man was once again given direct access to his Creator! What a celebration in heaven there must have been at that moment! Through Jesus, we can have the deep personal intimacy that Adam enjoyed with our Creator. How, then, are we to optimize this restored intimacy? In Matthew 6:6, Jesus tells us to go into our private closet to seek our Father's face. This secret unfettered worship of our Creator is a sweet incense before the throne of God (Revelation 5:8). Scripture says we are to seek God's face continuously (1 Chronicles 16:11). As King David wrote in Psalm 123, "I lift up my eyes unto Thee, O Thou who dwells in the Heavens." King David was larger than life in so many ways. His proclivity for unfettered praise and worship found in the Psalms is but one example of this incredible man's love for his Creator. David had an extraordinary ability to put his thoughts into writing, and when he kept his eyes affixed to heaven, he was "a man after God's own heart" (Acts 13:22). But King David was also a man of extremes, given to periods of darkness, and in those dark times, he was capable of great sin. David's life is a testament to all Christians. When we diligently seek after God, he will find us (Proverbs 8:17). Our hearts are not hidden from God, neither are our actions in this life. Hebrews 12:1 says that we are continuously surrounded by a great cloud of heavenly witnesses who rejoice when even one sinner repents (Luke 15:10). These scriptures bear witness that, even as earthbound souls, we are never separated from a God who sees all things. We were created for his pleasure (Revelation 4:11), and his pleasure resides in having a continuous relationship with us built on trust, love, obedience, and faith. He placed us on this Earth for that purpose, and his promise to us is his faithfulness and truth (Isaiah 25). Though our earthly eyes have been shuttered to the true glory of God's presence, we have the spirit of God living within us, and it is his promise to bring all things to our remembrance (John 14:26). May we listen diligently for his quiet reminding voice and seek after our heavenly Father with praise and thanksgiving.

Why Do Calamities Happen?

I recently attended the funeral of a former colleague of mine. He passed away suddenly and unexpectedly from a heart attack, leaving a wife and two daughters. My friend was only forty-nine years old. He was an educator and coach and was beloved in his community. My friend was also a Christian. Tragedies such as this strike at our emotions, filling our thoughts with unresolved questions and uncertainties. Constrained within our earthbound reasoning, we often find ourselves asking, "Why did this have to happen?" I think that Christians sometimes feel that God should exempt the faithful from the usual calamities that are common to man. It's true, that on the surface, the twenty-third Psalm seems to convey a feeling of "protection" from such dangers but that is an incorrect assumption. God does not promise an idyllic sheltered life from all storms, but he does promise to never leave or forsake us as we walk this path of life. The Book of Job stands in testament to that. The calamities that descended upon Job and his family were allowed to occur by God. That point is very clear in scripture. Sometimes seemingly bad things happen to Christians at the approval of heaven, and God may allow such difficulties for purposes completely unbeknownst to us at that moment. All bad things are the result of sin coming into the world through the beguiling hand of Satan, and we should never lose sight of the fact that Satan is the initiator of all such evil, as he roams the Earth as prince of this world. Fortunately, his time to disrupt is limited and so is the range of his ability. When the devil attacked Jesus in Matthew 4:1, he was thwarted on every point by Christ quoting the Word of God for his defense. Satan had no recourse but to flee from the Word in defeat. The Word of God (Bible) will always be our fortress when confronted with the calamities of this life. As King

David wrote in Psalm 57, "Yea, into the shadow of your wings I will make my refuge until these calamities pass me by." As the sons and daughters of Adam, we enter into an imperfect world, born into imperfect bodies. The miracle of flawless DNA replication sustains our bodies in youth but deteriorates in later years, leaving us vulnerable to diseases and health complications. Eventually, we all return to the Earth from whence we came (Ecclesiastes 12:7). As Christians, we live in faith that death has no sting, that to be absent from the body is to be present with the Lord (2 Corinthians 5:8). But death, when it comes unexpectedly, will always have a shock effect upon us. It is natural to feel this way, and we mourn the loss as a collective body. The world has no answer for these events, but Christians, through faith, know that "all things (including death) work together for good, to them that love God, who are the called according to his purpose" (Romans 8:28). When my friend died, hundreds of people's hearts were touched. Without doubt, his loss will be felt deeply by his family and all that loved him. But God had a purpose to take him from this Earth at the young age of forty-nine, and I suspect that reason had to do with someone else gaining eternal salvation through his passing. Rest in the arms of Jesus, my brother.

What Is the Essence of Faith?

What is the essence of faith? We often use the phrase, "Hey, I have faith in you," when generally, it means just the opposite—that we are not expecting the best outcome. Does our spiritual faith share a common thread with that? Hebrews 11:1 says, "Faith is the substance of things hoped for, the evidence of things not seen." We cannot see our heavenly Father, but as Christians, we believe that our Creator exists, and through that belief, we have the hope of eternal life through Jesus Christ, as promised to us in John 3:16. We cannot physically see God on his throne, but we are everywhere surrounded by the evidence of his creative hand (Romans 1:20). As Christians, we believe, by faith, that Jesus was resurrected from the dead and that through his resurrection, we have the gift of eternal life. The Apostle Paul writes in 1 Corinthians 15:17 that if Christ was not raised from the dead, our faith would be worthless. Therefore, our faith actually represents our personal trust in the promises of God. In the books of the Old Testament, written centuries before the birth of Christ, faith promises concerning Jesus abound. Those authors boldly prophesied the coming of the Messiah (Isaiah 9:6). Orthodox Jews today are still hanging onto those promises, waiting for the Messiah, even as they blindly overlook the obvious fulfillment of those prophesies in the birth of Jesus in Bethlehem, his early life, ministry, his death by crucifixion, and his glorious resurrection. These are all affirmations of the exact prophetic writings found in the Old Testament. Jesus, during his earthly ministry, repeatedly emphasized the importance of faith, blessing those who diligently sought after him. In Luke 18:42, he restored the blind man's sight because of his faith. In Matthew 8:5–13, Jesus marveled at the faith of the centurion (a gentile) who asked Jesus (a Jew) for his servant's healing.

In Matthew 17:20, when Jesus's disciples were unable to cast out a demon from a child, Jesus rebuked them for their sparsity of faith, saying, "If ye had faith the size of a grain of mustard seed, you could move mountains." In Matthew 9:21–22, the woman with an issue of blood for twelve years said to herself, "If I can just touch the hem of Jesus's garment, I shall be healed." What faith that took on her part! We should all seek after God with that same degree of confidence in the outcome of our endeavors. Colossians 2:12 says that "we are risen with him through faith in the operation of God, who hath raised him from the dead." God's "operation" never changes. It is the same yesterday, today, and forever (Hebrews 13:8), whereby we can have total assurance in the Lord as our loving shepherd, even as the storms of this life swirl around us. Whether we are in crisis mode or in calm waters, Jesus on Calvary's cross tore open the curtain veil to the Holy of Holies (Matthew 15:38), whereby we now may enter and cry, "Abba, Father," boldly approaching the throne of grace knowing, through faith, that God is listening to us (Hebrews 4:16).

The Mystery of the Holy Spirit

In 1 Corinthians 2:7–10, the Apostle Paul says that he speaks the wisdom of God in a mystery, even the hidden wisdom, which God ordained before the ages. God has revealed these hidden things of himself through his Spirit, who searches all things and assists us in our spiritual understanding. The natural (unsaved) man cannot comprehend these spiritual mysteries, and therefore, they appear as foolishness to him (verse 14). In the Bible, the Holy Spirit is introduced in Genesis 1:1 in the phrase "in the beginning God." The word chosen for "God" is Elohim, which describes the plurality of God (Father, Son, and Holy Spirit), or in church vernacular, the Holy Trinity. The Holy Spirit is specifically named in verse 2, where it says, "And the Spirit of God moved upon the face of the waters." The term "Holy Spirit" is the English derivative of the Hebrew term used in the books of the Old Testament. The New Testament, however, was written in Greek, and the English translation, which occurred in 1600 AD by King James, advocated for the term "Holy Ghost." The terms are interchangeable, and most modern printings favor the use of Holy Spirit. Jesus in John 15:26 instructed his disciples on the coming of the Holy Spirit as he prepared them for the time after his death. He described the Holy Spirit as the "comforter" who would be sent by the Father after his resurrection and will "guide you in all truth" (John 16:13). Through scripture (John 16:8, 2 Peter 3:9), we know that a chief mandate of the Holy Spirit is conviction of sin in the unbeliever with a desire to bring all men to repentance. This sincere act of repentance unto salvation triggers a miraculous event, where God, in the person of the Holy Spirit, resides within us. The second major work of the Holy Spirit involves his daily guidance for believers on the path to spiritual maturity and sanctification.

This cleansing (of worldly lifestyle) is centered on our recognition of carnal behaviors, which create barriers in our communication with God. The early Christian churches were often subject to these types of mistakes in doctrine and lifestyle. Contentions frequently arose in early congregations over who should receive the spiritual gifts of the Holy Spirit described by Apostle Paul in 1 Corinthians 12:8. These "gifts" are often referred to as baptisms of the Holy Spirit. Prior to 1850, most Christian churches believed that the "baptism of the Holy Spirit" occurred at conversion, or during the rites of Christian initiation, and generally, there were no outward signs of an indwelling Spirit. The "Holiness movement" of 1850s broke out of this morass by elevating the role of the Holy Spirit in the life of the believer. This was followed by the Pentecostal movement in the 1920s and the "Charismatic" or "Jesus movement" of the 1970s, where enormous emphasis was placed on the manifestation of spiritual "gifts" as a sign of having received the "baptism of the Holy Spirit." The book of Acts records the effects of this baptism on the disciples (Acts 2:2) and the raw evangelistic power, which was released in spreading the message of Christ by those who received the baptism of the Holy Spirit. As the apostles traveled and preached to new congregations, they would frequently ask, "Whose baptism have ye received?" The answer was usually "by water," whereupon the apostles would either pray or lay hands on them to receive the baptism of the Holy Spirit (Acts 11:15, Acts 19:6). This "second baptism" was seen as significant by the apostles and was acknowledged in their picking of Stephen in Acts 6:5.

The Mystery of the Holy Spirit (Continued)

The spiritual gifts described by Apostle Paul in 1 Corinthians chapter 12 have been at the forefront of all of the famous Pentecostal movements in church history. These gifts fall into categories such as wisdom, knowledge, faith, healing, working of miracles, prophesy, discerning of spirits, speaking in tongues, and the interpretation of tongues. Each of these gifts are associated with having received the baptism of the Holy Spirit and are given for the edification of the church. Positions of authority in the congregation are also determined and set in place by God (verse 28). In chapter 13, Paul reveals that while having these gifts from the Holy Spirit is desirable, the greatest spiritual attribute we should seek is love. Love encompasses all of the other fruits of the Spirit, and unlike some of the gifts, love will not go away (verse 8). Paul explains in chapter 14 that the Holy Spirit provides spiritual gifts for two purposes, i.e., self-edification, as in speaking in tongues, which benefits only the user (verse 4), and church edification, which benefits the congregation as a whole (verse 12). Paul also warns that overzealous use of spiritual gifts in the church can lead to a chaotic environment for worship. God is not the author of confusion but of peace, decency, and order (verse 33). There have been times, however, when God felt the need to shake things up a bit by pouring out his Spirit in what has often been called "awakenings." During these periods of intense spiritual revival, the presence of the Holy Spirit is magnified in many unusual ways through the open exhibition of spiritual gifts upon the members of the gatherings. Healings, unknown tongues being spoken, worshipers being "slain in the spirit" with shaking, trembling, and prostration on the floor, periods of "holy hush" when total silence descends on the congregation, and even more gregarious behaviors such as dancing and leaping, "holy laughter," and feelings of electricity through the body, are commonplace occurrences. In the past two hundred years, several of these intense prolonged outpourings have occurred across the globe. In 1904, there was the great Welsh Revival, followed by the Azusa Street Revival in 1906 in Los Angeles. The Toronto Awakening occurred in Canada in 1994, followed by the Brownsville Church Revival in Pensacola, Florida, from 1995 through 2000. Each of these events was characterized by very unusual manifestations of the Holy Spirit and lasting several years. These "awakenings" have had a profound effect on the body of Christ through the experiences of conviction of sin, repentance, regeneration, spiritual joy, and the salvation of thousands of people. Oswald Chambers, the author of *My Utmost for His Highest*, after attending a revival in 1907, defined the joy he experienced as the "perfect fulfillment for which we were created and regenerated." These "awakenings" by the Holy Spirit seem to jumpstart the world's spiritual battery. The dry theological rust is knocked off, the pipes are cleared out, and the spirit of believers is strengthened for the long haul. Romans 15:13 says, "Now the God of hope fill you with all joy and peace in believing, that you may abound in hope, through the power of the Holy Spirit." It is through the power of the indwelling Holy Spirit that we, as believers, are lifted up into the presence of our Father and, through intercession for us, makes our praise and petitions known unto God.

Reconciliation

In 2 Corinthians 5:18, the Apostle Paul says that "God has reconciled us to Himself through Jesus Christ." Reconciliation is the act of reuniting or bringing together again people or parties that have been in disagreement. There are approximately 4,200 religions in the world, and outside Christianity, the word "reconciliation" between man and God does not apply. In most world religions, attempts are made to appease the "deity figure" through strict adherence to ritualistic behaviors of worship. There is very little in the way of "relationship," as all spiritual energy flows in one direction (toward the deity). In Christianity, however, "reconciliation" is central to God's overall theme. From Genesis to Revelation, the writers of the Bible, under the guidance of the Holy Spirit, have unveiled God's incredible plan for restoring man to the garden of Eden. The garden was the initial setting for God's love relationship with Adam and Eve. The book of Genesis does not allude to the length of time Adam and Eve lived like this—in perfect bodies and in perfect harmony with their Creator. It may have been millions of years, possibly billions of years, but eventually, Satan, whose solitary purpose has always been to drive enmity between man and God, initiated the temptation in Eve to disobey. Our first parents willingly chose that which was forbidden by God, and, in doing so, introduced the first human sins into the world. Adam and Eve's disobedience destroyed the unity they had with God and with his Creation, and their sin brought death and spiritual separation to a previously perfect world (Romans 6:23). Beginning with their children, Cain and Abel, God set forth his requirements (Genesis 4:3) for sin offerings that would culminate four thousand years later on the cross at Calvary. In the Old Testament times, the sins of the people were forgiven once a year by the high priest entering into the temple holy of holies to present a blood sacrifice. The people themselves were not allowed to come into the presence of God in the inner temple room. This was an incomplete form of reconciliation, and would remain so, until Jesus's death on the cross tore open the veil in the temple that separated man from God (Matthew 27:51). Christ was the ultimate love gift of reconciliation from a holy God and was the only form of redemption that God the Father could accept for atonement of man's sin. If we prayerfully contemplate just what this sacrifice by Jesus meant to the Father, we should all fall fearfully prostrate before his throne in shame for our sins. At the Brownsville Awakening in 1995, I witnessed this awful "awareness of sin" fall on people, frequently placing them prostrate on the ground in guilt and repentance. Sin is a terrible thing to a Holy God. Only the blood of Jesus could fully reconcile man to himself. That is the *power* in the words used in John 3:16, "For God so loved the world, that He *gave* His only begotten Son, that whosoever believeth in him, should not perish, but have everlasting life." It is through this truth that the ministry of the "good news" is preached throughout the world that forgiveness of sin (reconciliation) is only possible through Jesus Christ our Lord (John 14:6).

Can Prayer Alter God's Will?

In recent discussions, I was asked if I thought prayer could alter the will of God. It is an interesting question, and as with most theological inquiries, there are differing views. 1 Thessalonians 5:17 instructs us to pray without ceasing. James 5:16 says that "the effectual fervent prayer of a righteous man availeth much," and Luke 18:1 states that "men ought always to pray." Prayer is our pathway to the throne of God. We are therefore instructed, as followers of Jesus, to use prayer as a platform of worship and petition to God (Philippians 4:6). Herein lies the conundrum. If we believe that God's plans and purposes are immutable (preordained), do our prayers really have the ability to move God in another direction? The Reformed or Calvinistic view of prayer has God's immutable will at the fore and is decidedly different from the doctrinal teaching of the Armenian and Charismatic churches, where man's free will is center stage in an understanding of God's plan. There is no doubt that God's sovereignty stands immutable. Hebrews 13:8–9 tells us that Jesus Christ is the same yesterday, today, and forever. Malachi 3:6 says, "For I am the Lord, I changeth not," and in James 1:17, the Lord tells us that "every good gift is from above, and cometh down from the Father, with whom there is no variableness or shadow of turning." God created all things, and he created them for his own pleasure (Revelation 4:11). God's providential plan for mankind cannot be altered. Neither can we impose upon God's ultimate strategy for the end-time. Therefore, we should not pray in an attempt to ask God to alter his plans, nor should our prayers be directed to move God from his purposes. Our prayers should be a reflection of our own weaknesses, and our dependency on him for all good things, lifting our voices in holy worship as we present our requests (Phillipians

4:6). In Matthew 7:7–8 Jesus instructed us to "ask" that we may receive. We have faith that God will providentially care for our basic requirements of food and clothing as he does for the lilies of the field and the fowls of the air (Matthew 6:33), but more importantly, Jesus spoke of prayer with respect to the kingdom of God. In furtherance, Jesus instructs us in John 16:23 to make our requests in his name. Praying in Jesus's name is to ask for Christ's approval. This is a significant qualifier for our prayer requests. Our petitions must be aligned to further God's kingdom, and if they are, he will always hear us (1 John 5:14). Such is the case that, too often in our prayers, we ask "amiss," and when we do, we will not receive (James 5:4). Prayers for the physical healing of others is appropriate and is encouraged in scripture (James 5:14, Acts 28:8); however, our prayers do not guarantee their recovery. To receive healing, it must be in accordance with God's will for them. The Apostle Paul came to understand this after being repeatedly denied in his request to have a physical infirmity removed from him (2 Corinthians 12:8–9). It was simply not in God's will to do so. People often ask if prayers for personal prosperity or abundance are proper. James 4:3 warns us that prayer requests will be "amiss" if not in proper alignment with God's will. If God perceives that our asking for prosperity will place us in Satan's snare in regards to coveting money (1 Timothy 6:9–10), then it would not be surprising if that request was denied. It is certain that God, who searches our hearts (Romans 8:27), discerns our abilities to receive gifts, and on this basis, to some he may give ten talents, and to some he gives one talent (Matthew 25:14). In light of these scriptures, the name-it-and-claim-it prosperity doctrine presented by some popular TV evangelists may run in opposition to the true meaning of Christ's teachings. Jesus never elevated the pursuit of prosperity, nor did his disciples promote wealth as a reward for following Christ. Only God knows what

Can Prayer Alter God's Will (Continued)

truly lies in each of our hearts. We know through Matthew chapter 6 that it is in God's will for our needs to be met, but verse 33 says, "Seek ye first the Kingdom of God and His righteousness, and all these things shall be added unto you." How often do we consider the kingdom of God when we come before our heavenly Father in prayers of petition? If I may quote Arthur W. Pink (1886–1956), "Prayer is the Divinely appointed means, whereby we may obtain from God the things we ask, providing we ask for those things which are in accord with His Will." With that said, we return to our original question: Can prayer alter the will of God? If we believe that God's will is a singular eternal decree, the answer is probably "no." However, scripture reveals many instances where our heavenly Father "turned from, or relented" terms, which to seem to indicate a willingness on God's part to "negotiate" with man where circumstances allow. It is in God's pleasure to have an intimate relationship with man, whereby even the smallest concerns of our lives are openly and prayerfully considered before his throne. We come before our heavenly Father in faith that he is as a concerning parent, who has "personal involvement" in our prayer requests, and in the sure and certain hope that El Shaddai, our mother/father God, loves us, cares for our well-being, and leads us to still waters in this life and the life to come.

Carnality and the Cross

As Christians, we are admonished in scripture to put off the "old man." So what does this mean? The Apostle Paul preached tirelessly on the subject of "transformation." "Be ye transformed by the renewing of your mind" (Romans 12:2). Paul was speaking of sanctification, the casting off of sinful behaviors. In the early church, there was a desire by some to retain many of the old sinful ways. Paul recognized this false practice and admonished the believers in Rome on the spiritual dangers of living carnally (Romans chapter 6). In 1 Peter 1:16, we are commanded by our heavenly Father to be holy even as he is holy by the "throwing off" of carnal behaviors. The same human frailties that were found in the believers at Rome are resident in our hearts today and must be recognized and purged in order to walk in sanctification. In the Old Testament, the Lord used visual incentives to spiritually energize the children of Israel, but even when guided by a pillar of fire in the wilderness, or walking through a divided Red Sea, God's people still fell back into old sinful behaviors. A thousand years later, during the time of Jesus's ministry, these same vagrancies of the human spirit were evident in his disciples. Jesus knew of the coming persecutions and the mass killings of Christians for their faith, and he was well aware of his disciple's weaknesses when faced with fear. To counteract this, Jesus asked for a "holy anointing" (John 14:16). His gifting of the Holy Spirit to dwell within us and guide us in our spiritual pilgrimage aligns perfectly with Psalm 23:3, where "He leads us in the paths of righteousness, for his name's sake." The Holy Spirit illuminates our path, but he does not force us to make the correct choices. That responsibility is ours alone through the exercise of our free will. Psalm 14 says, "Let the words of my mouth and the meditations of my heart, be acceptable in thy sight, O lord." How difficult this is without the assistance from the Holy Spirit. Our minds are often caught up with the loud distractions of life in this social media world. The Holy Spirit does not shout but speaks in a quiet inner voice that takes discipline to hear. So why should we make this "transforming" process a priority? When Jesus was nailed on Calvary's cross, he bore the entire sin load of the world, from Adam's first sin to mine and yours right now. The physical pain of crucifixion was horrific, but the spiritual disgust of carrying this enormous sin load twisted his physical countenance to such a degree that he became almost unrecognizable as a human being (Isaiah 52:14). This repulsive burden was so loathsome that Christ briefly felt his heavenly Father turn away. What unimaginable horror that must have been! But he bore that weight and paid the atonement price demanded by heaven for a total reconciliation with our heavenly Father. As he took his last breath, Jesus shouted, "It is finished!," and with that exclamation, the temple curtain was torn from top to bottom in the holy of holies, providing for the first time, since the garden of Eden, personal access for all of us to the throne of God. That burden of sin on the cross was ours to suffer for, but Jesus, in his infinite love, took that from us. Our sins that Christ bore on the cross two thousand years ago were sins we commit today. As Christians, we should all feel a great responsibility for placing that burden on Christ. The Apostle Paul felt the weight of that responsibility when he exclaimed in Romans 7:19–24, "For the good I would do, I do not, but the evil which I would not, that I do. Oh, wretched man that I am." May we each seek to throw off the "old sinful man" with the assistance of the Holy Spirit and enter as "regenerated" into the glory and presence of Christ.

Spiritual Joy

In Galatians chapter 5, the Apostle Paul describes the fruits of the Spirit. These are characteristics of human behavior, which may be reflected in the persona of Christians through the inner working of the Holy Spirit. In earlier *Musings* pages, I have briefly discussed "peace" and "faith," which are also fruits of Spirit. Now we will look at the aspect of "spiritual joy," and how this fruit may be expressed in the lives of believers. The words "joy" and "rejoice" are used over 356 times in the Bible. Philippians 4:4 says, "Rejoice in the Lord always, again I say Rejoice." When Paul wrote of joy, he used the Greek word that refers to a feeling of gratitude and thankfulness to God. Spiritual joy floods the hearts of believers when they contemplate an eternal life in the presence of God's glory and majesty. "Rejoice because your names are written in heaven" (Luke 10:20). Isaiah 12:3 says, "Therefore with *joy* shall you draw water from the well of salvation." Joy flourishes when we follow in the footsteps of Jesus, whose commandment to love one another permeates every aspect of our lives. Spiritual joy requires that we step away from our self-centered lives and enter an environment of sharing with others. In contrast to happiness, which is an emotion that comes and goes according to earthly circumstances, spiritual joy is often manifested even in the worst of times (Romans 5:3). In 1 Thessalonians 1:6, Paul describes our joy as being Spirit-given, and through his intervention, we can be assured that we may experience the fullness of joy in our prayer life (Psalm 16:11). Joy is forward-looking. Most Christians experience a sense of joy in songs of praise such as "Amazing Grace," whose verses explore the exceedingly great and precious promises for our future (2 Peter 1:4). One of the great mistakes made by the Christian church over the centuries has been in the area of frowning upon outward signs of joy in church services. Joy bashing through church policies prohibiting dancing, the raising of hands or voices, use of modern musical instruments, and other outward signs of joy in the church has long infiltrated church dogma. However, an examination of scripture both in the Old and New Testaments points to a different position on this subject. Psalm 98:4 says, "Make a joyful noise unto the Lord," referring to any pure outpouring of joyful expression before God. King David danced before the Lord in joy (2 Samuel 6:14). Intense spiritual joy with displays of clapping, dancing, raising of hands, and music has been one of the more obvious manifestations of the Holy Spirit during the great revivals of this century, and in Acts chapter 2, the Apostles were accused of being drunk when they expressed Spirit-filled joy following the Pentecost outpouring. All Christians experience some form of spiritual joy in their lives, even under the most trying of circumstances. May our joy be a reflection of Romans 15:13, which says, "Now the God of hope fill you with all joy and peace in believing, that ye may abound in hope, through the power of the Holy Spirit." *Amen.*

The Gift of Israel

The land of Israel holds a special place in God's heart. In Genesis 12:2, God selected Abraham to be the father of a great nation, and from this nation (verse 3), "all the families of the earth would be blessed." Abraham was instructed by God to move to the land of Canaan (modern-day Israel), where God said, "Unto thy seed will I give this land forever" (Genesis 13:15). This is the Abrahamic covenant, a permanent and eternal land gift from our heavenly Father to his chosen people, a people who would share a common heritage over the next four thousand years. The majority of the books of the Old Testament deal with the establishment and governance of the twelve tribes of Israel in Canaan (Palestine), the establishment of Jerusalem as capitol, and the construction of the temple. Old Testament books also document several diaspora (exile) of Jews from Israel as captives of invading armies. At the time when Jesus was born in Bethlehem, Israel was a conquered nation under the supervision of Rome. Later in 70 AD, when the temple was finally destroyed, much of the Jewish population had already scattered throughout Asia Minor and Italy. The final diaspora of the Jews from Palestine occurred in 132 AD, when Rome crushed the last Jewish revolt and drove them from their land. For the last two thousand years, Christians and Jews have been waiting for God to fulfill his promise to return the Jewish people to the land of Israel from their scatterings around the world. This "aliyah," or "return to the land of Israel," is prophesied in Isaiah 11:11, Deuteronomy 30:3, Ezekiel 37:21–21 and 28:25, and Jeremiah 23:3,8. The entire sequence of events surrounding the 2nd coming of Christ, including the rapture of the church (1 Thessalonians 4:13–18), the seven years of tribulation, and the battle of Armageddon, are predicated on the return of the Jews to the land of Israel. This incredible prophesy was fulfilled on May 14, 1948, with the official declaration of the State of Israel by David Ben-Gurion, their first political leader. Prior to this, the land of Palestine was under the control of British Mandate following WWII, and Jewish immigration was illegal because of the increasing violence with the existing Arab population. Leon Uris's best-selling book, *Exodus*, documents this difficult and hazardous journey, taken surreptitiously by hundreds of thousands of Holocaust survivors trying to get to their ancestral homeland between 1945 and 1947. After Israel's independence was declared in 1948, Jewish repatriation to Palestine was swift. Over one million Jews from all over war-torn Europe completed their aliyah to Israel between 1948 and 1950. The surrounding Arab nations vehemently objected to this massive influx of Jews with frequent and violent uprisings. In an attempt to stop the violence, the United Nations brokered an armistice agreement in 1949, setting territorial boundaries in Palestine. This was the beginning of the diplomatic attempt to create a two-state solution, which continues today. The Six-Day War fought in 1967 between Israel and most of the surrounding Arab countries ended in a stunning victory for Israel, significantly increasing Israel's land holdings. More importantly, through their military victory, the Jewish people gained access to western parts of Jerusalem, including the sacred West Wall (Wailing Wall) of the Temple Mount. This was their first ownership of that most sacred place in almost two thousand years. In 1973, violence once again erupted in the Holy Land with the Yom Kippur War between Israel and Egypt and Syria. This conflict ended after months of intense warfare with territorial gains for Israel in the Sinai and the Golan Heights. Throughout the past seventy years of Israel's independence, there have been many attempts at brokering peace agreements in the Mideast. All have failed to produce a lasting resolution to the conflict. The tensions between Arabs and Jews extend back four thousand years to the time of Abraham when he fathered two sons from different mothers. His first son, Ishmael, was

The Gift of Israel (Continued)

the child of Hagar, the Egyptian handmaiden of Abraham's wife, Sarah. It was thought that Sarah could no longer bear children because of her age, and so she allowed Abraham to marry Hagar to bear him a son. When God finally blessed the womb of Sarah, she bore Isaac, in whom God chose to establish his covenant (Genesis 17:19), thus placing Isaac in the direct lineage leading to Christ. God did not forget Hagar, and he blessed Ishmael to "be the father of a great nation" (Genesis 17:20). It should be noted that the religion of Islam believes that Abraham is their father and acknowledges that Isaac is the father of the Jews. This Israeli-Arab relationship, however strained, is one ordained by God with blessings given to both Isaac and Ishmael. It is unfortunate, however, given the warning by God in Genesis 12:3, that the Arab nations have chosen to fight Israel. The military defeat of these nations in the end-time is prophesied in the books of Ezekiel and Revelation. As for the United States, we are currently Israel's closest ally in both financial and military support, but political affiliations are fickle and can change drastically over the course of one presidential election. It is my fervent prayer that America will continue to support Israel, for it is far better to receive blessings than curses. God's sovereign will is not constrained by the errant winds of political ideology. Therefore, we must continue to pray, as directed in Psalm 122:6, for "the peace of Jerusalem; for they shall prosper who love thee." Amen.

Final Thoughts

The writing of *Musings of a Persecuted Soul* has been a spiritual catharsis for me. I began *Musings* as a release mechanism for the persecution I felt in my soul. I was having faith issues in trying to find balance between my Christian training and beliefs and my secular education and personal observations. As a Christian, I felt I should be able to reach a certain level of spiritual equilibrium about the things of God and the natural world around me. In 2013, I took a step of faith and began my quest to find the answers in scripture. I kept an ear open for the gentle whisperings of the Holy Spirit, which is promised in Hebrews 4:12, "The Word of God is living, and powerful, and sharper than any two-edged sword; and is a discerner of the thoughts and intents of the heart." My intentions were honorable. I needed to find the spiritual equilibrium, which would counteract the cynicism I so often felt. Over the course of the last several years, I know that God honored my quest with patience and gentleness, as he has often done throughout my life. Because I am a firm believer in "free will" as it applies to our earthly decisions, and ultimately, to our eternal life or death, I felt God would bless my good faith endeavor with some degree of elucidation on these issues. I was correct in that assumption but only as it applies to myself. Many of the positions I take are debatable (maybe even deplorable) to others with differing views, and I humbly accept that I may be completely wrong on any of my points of theological dogma. I began writing *Musings of a Persecuted Soul* for my own personal edification, and the Lord was gracious and long-suffering with my feeble attempts at probing the mysteries of heaven. I still remain a firm believer in premillennial end-time with Israel's dominant position in world events leading up to the rapture. I am committed to my belief that the geologic history of the Earth is billions of years old and that dinosaurs roamed our planet long before God created Adam and Eve. These beliefs come from my personal observations and from my interpretation of scripture. I have also come to the realization that not all of God's mysteries are open to man's examination, and I humbly yield on that point. Throughout my writings, I have remained cognizant of God's explicit warning, both in the Old Testament (Proverbs 30:6) and in the New Testament (Revelation 22:18–19), not to change the words of scripture for one's personal benefit, and I have tried to tread lightly when exploring areas of established theological doctrine. With that said, I also contend that God grants us the freedom to explore his precepts and his wonderful works of creation with open minds and open hearts. *Musings of a Persecuted Soul* is the story of my personal quest for answers. Through its creation, my love for God has deepened, and my awareness of his mercy and grace upon my life has heightened. Through the researching and writing process of *Musings*, the Holy Spirit has given me my spiritual equilibrium. I pray that you might find the same blessing in God's Word as I did. Peace be with you.

M. A. Ewing

About the Author

Mr. Ewing is a retired public school administrator from the State of Florida. After receiving his degree in zoology from the University of Iowa in 1976, Mr. Ewing embarked on a sixteen-year teaching career in the life sciences at both middle and high school levels. In 1994, with a master's degree in educational leadership, he began a second career in public school administration, serving in positions of assistant principal, principal, and district coordinator, before retiring in 2013. As a lifelong Christian, Mr. Ewing often found himself in juxtaposition between established church ideologies and his scientific observations of the natural world. Over time, these nagging questions began to foster a growing cynicism toward areas of the Bible, which appeared to conflict with modern scientific understanding. He also found that these Biblical conundrums are rarely discussed among Christians, or from the church pulpit. Faced with growing faith issues, the author embraced Acts 17:10–11, where Apostle Paul praised the Bereans for "searching the scriptures for truth." Following in their example, the author began an exhaustive scriptural investigation, searching for spiritual equilibrium between his scientific training and his faith. It was through this heartfelt search for elucidation that *Musings of a Persecuted Soul* was born. Hebrews 4:12 states that the Word of God is a "discerner of the thoughts and intents of the heart." Over the course of the author's scriptural investigation, the Holy Spirit worked a cleansing miracle on the cynicism that had so encrusted his soul. God's truth, sharper than any two-edged sword, pierced through the scale and doubt that had built up over decades, revealing the spiritual peace and equilibrium he had so long desired.

CPSIA information can be obtained
at www.ICGtesting.com
Printed in the USA
FSHW011707050121
77399FS